# NAVIGATION FOR THE AMATEUR

A MANUAL ON TRADITIONAL NAVIGATION ON
WATER AND LAND BY STAR
AND SUN OBSERVATION

BY **E. T. MORTON**
ORIGINALLY PUBLISHED IN 1912

---

## LEGACY EDITION

THE CLASSIC OUTING HANDBOOKS COLLECTION
BOOK 19

Doublebit Press

*New content, introduction, cover design, and annotations
Copyright © 2021 by Doublebit Press. All rights reserved.
www.doublebitpress.com | Cherry, IL, USA*

*Originally published in 1912 by E. T. Morton.
Doublebit Press Legacy Edition ISBNs
Hardcover: 978-1-64389-194-1
Paperback: 978-1-64389-195-8*

*WARNING: Some of the material in this book may be outdated by modern safety standards. This antique text may contain outdated and unsafe information, recreational activities, projects, or mechanical, electrical, chemical, or medical practices. Any use of this book for purposes other than historic study may result in unsafe and hazardous conditions and individuals act at their own risk and are responsible for their own safety. Doublebit Press, its authors, or its agents assume no liability for any injury, harm, or damages to persons or property arising either directly or indirectly from any content contained in this text or the activities performed by readers. Remember to be safe with any activity or work you do and use good judgement by following proper health and safety protocols. In addition, because this book was from a past time and is presented in an unabridged form, the contents may be culturally or racially insensitive. Such content does not represent the opinions or positions of the publisher and are presented for historical posterity and accuracy to the original text.*

*DISCLAIMER: Doublebit Press has not tested or analyzed the methods, materials, and practices appearing in this public domain text and provides no warranty to the accuracy and reliability of the content. This text is provided only as a reprinted facsimile from the unedited public domain original as first published and authored. This text is published for historical study and personal literary enrichment purposes only. The publisher assumes no liability for any injury, harm, or damages to persons or property arising either directly or indirectly from any information contained within or activities performed by readers.*

# INTRODUCTION
## To The Doublebit Press Legacy Edition

The old experts of the woods, mountains, and farm country life taught timeless principles and skills for decades. Through their books, the old experts offered rich descriptions of the outdoor world and encouraged learning through personal experiences in nature. Over the last 125 years, handcrafts, artisanal works, outdoors activities, and our experiences with nature have substantially changed. Many things have gotten simpler as equipment and processes have improved, and life outside, on the farm, or on the trail now brings with it many of the same comforts enjoyed in town. In addition, some activities of the old days are now no longer in vogue, or are even outright considered inappropriate or illegal. However, despite many of the positive changes in handcrafting, traditional skills, and outdoors methods that have occurred over the years, *there are many other skills and much knowledge that are at risk of being lost* that should never be forgotten.

By publishing Legacy Editions of classic texts on handcrafts, artisanal skills, nature lore, survival, and outdoors and camping life, it is our goal at Doublebit Press to do what we can to preserve and share the works from forgotten teachers that form the cornerstone of the authentic and hard-wrought American tradition of self-sustainability and self-reliance. Through remastered reprint editions of timeless classics of traditional crafts, classic methods, and outdoor recreation, perhaps we can regain some of this lost knowledge for future generations.

On the frontier, folks made virtually everything by hand. Old farmers' knowledge and homestead skills were passed on to the future generation because it meant survival. In addition, much of traditional handcrafts and outdoors life knowledge was passed on from American Indians – the original handcrafters and outdoorsmen of the Americas.

Today, much of the handcrafted items of the frontier are made in factories, only briefly seeing a human during the process (if at all). Making things by hand indeed takes much (often strenuous) work, but it provides an extreme sense of pride in the finished job. Instantly, all hand-made items come with a story on their creation. Most importantly, though, making items with traditional methods gives you experience and knowledge of how things work.

This is similar to the case of camping and the modern outdoors experience, with neatly arranged campsites at public campgrounds and camping gear that has been meticulously improved and tested in both the lab and the field. These changes have also caused us to lose this traditional knowledge, having it buried in the latest high-tech iteration of your latest camp gadget.

Many modern conveniences are only a brief trek away, with many parks, campgrounds, and even forests having easy-access roads, convenience stores, and even cell phone signal. In some ways, it is much easier to camp and go outdoors today, and that is a good thing! We should not be miserable when we go outside — lovers of the outdoors know the essential restorative capability that the woods can have on the body, mind, and soul. But to experience it, you need to not be surrounded by modern high-tech robotic coffee pots, tents that build themselves, or watches that tell you how to do everything!

Although things have gotten easier on us in the 21st Century when it comes to handcrafts and the outdoors, it certainly does not mean that we should forget the foundations of technical skills, artisanal production, and outdoors lore. All of the modern tools and cool gizmos that make our lives easier are all founded on principles of traditional methods that the old masters knew well and taught to those who would listen. We just have to look deeply into the design of our modern gadgets and factories to see the original methods and traditional skills at play.

Every woods master and artisan had their own curriculum or thought some things were more important than others. The old masters also taught common things in slightly different ways or did things differently than others. That's what makes each of the experts different and worth reading. There's no universal way of doing something, especially today. Learning to go about something differently helps with mastery or learn a new skill altogether. Basically, you learn intimately how things work, giving you great skill with adapting and being flexible when the need arises.

Again, to use the metaphor from the above paragraphs, traditional skills mastery consists of learning the basic building blocks of how and why the old artisans made things, how they lived outdoors, and why woods and nature lore mattered. Everything is intertwined, and doing it by hand increases your knowledge of this complex network. Each master goes about describing these building blocks differently or shows a different aspect of them.

Therefore, we have decided to publish this Legacy Edition reprint in our collection of traditional handcraft and outdoors life classics. This book is an important contribution to the early American traditional skills and outdoors literature, and has important historical and collector value toward preserving the American tradition of self-sufficiency and artisan production. The knowledge it holds is an invaluable reference for practicing outdoors skills and hand craft methods. Its chapters thoroughly discuss some of the essential building blocks of knowledge that are fundamental but may have been forgotten as equipment gets fancier and technology gets smarter. In short, this book was chosen for Legacy Edition printing because much of the basic skills and knowledge it contains has been forgotten or put to the wayside in trade for more modern conveniences and methods.

Although the editors at Doublebit Press are thrilled to have comfortable experiences in the woods and love our modern equipment for making cool hand-made projects, we are also realizing that the basic skills taught by the old masters are more essential than ever as our culture becomes more and more hooked on digital stuff. We don't want to risk forgetting the important steps, skills, or building blocks involved with each step of traditional methods. Sometimes, *there's no substitute for just doing something on your own, by hand.* Sometimes, to truly learn something is to *just do it by hand.* The Legacy Edition series represents the essential contributions to the American handcraft and outdoors tradition by the great experts.

With technology playing a major role in everyday life, sometimes we need to take a step back in time to find those basic building blocks used for gaining mastery – the things that we have luckily not completely lost and has been recorded in books over the last two centuries. These skills aren't forgotten, they've just been shelved. *It's time to unshelve them once again and reclaim the lost knowledge of self-sufficiency.*

Based on this commitment to preserving our outdoors and handcraft heritage, we have taken great pride in publishing this book as a complete original work without any editorial changes or revisions. We hope it is worthy of both study and collection by handcrafters and outdoors folk in the modern era and to fulfill its status as a Legacy Edition by passing along to the libraries of future generations.

Unlike many other low-resolution photocopy reproductions of classic books that are common on the market, this Legacy Edition does not simply place poor photography of old texts on our pages and use error-prone optical scanning or computer-generated text. We want our work to speak for itself and reflect the quality demanded by our customers who spend their hard-earned money. With this in mind, each Legacy Edition book that has been chosen for publication is carefully remastered from original print books, *with the Doublebit Legacy Edition printed and laid out in the exact way that it was presented at its original publication.* Our Legacy Edition books are inspired by the original covers of first-edition texts, embracing the beauty that is in both the simplicity and sometimes ornate decoration of vintage and antique books. We want provide a beautiful, memorable experience that is as true to the original text as best as possible, but with the aid of modern technology to make as meaningful a reading experience as possible for books that are typically over a century old.

Because of its age and because it is presented in its original form, the book may contain misspellings, inking errors, and other print blemishes that were common for the age. However, these are exactly the things that we feel give the book its character, which we preserved in this Legacy Edition. During digitization, we did our best to ensure that each illustration in the text was clean and sharp with the least amount of loss from being copied and digitized as possible. Full-page plate illustrations are presented as they were found, often including the extra blank page that was often behind a plate and plate pagination. For the covers, we use the original cover design as our template to give the book its original feel. We are sure you'll appreciate the fine touches and attention to detail that your Legacy Edition has to offer.

For traditional handcrafters and outdoors enthusiasts who demand the best from their equipment, this Doublebit Press Legacy Edition reprint was made with you in mind. Both important and minor details have equally both been accounted for by our publishing staff, down to the cover, font, layout, and images. It is the goal of Doublebit Legacy Edition series to preserve America's handcrafting and outdoors heritage, but also be cherished as collectible pieces, worthy of collection in any person's library and that can be passed to future generations.

Every book selected to be in this series offers unique views and instruction on important skills, advice, tips, tidbits, anecdotes, stories, and experiences that will enrich the repertoire of any person looking to learn the skills it contains. To learn the most basic building blocks leads to mastery of all its aspects.

# NAVIGATION FOR THE AMATEUR

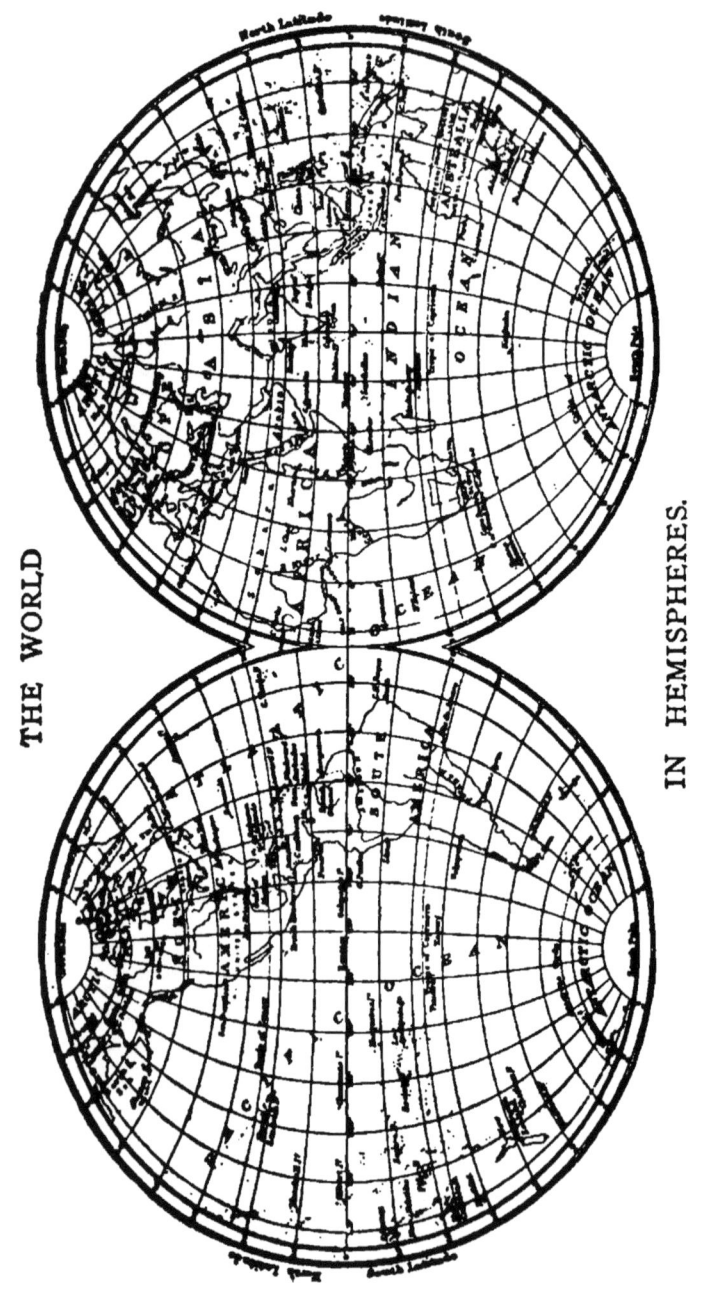

# NAVIGATION FOR THE AMATEUR

BY

CAPTAIN E. T. MORTON

*Illustrated with Diagrams*

Copyright, 1912, By
OUTING PUBLISHING COMPANY.

All rights reserved.

# PREFACE

In compiling this little hand-book on the simpler forms of Navigation, it has not been my intention to get up a treatise on the subject. This has already been done, and it would seem that there is hardly room for another comprehensive work on this subject. There are, however, a great many yachtsmen who desire to cruise off shore, and in order to do so want a little more navigation than they have heretofore mastered. Most of these do not care to go into the subject too deeply, being content with the simpler formulae for finding a ship's position by an altitude of the various heavenly bodies used in navigation. These formulae I have given with enough explanation to enable the amateur to understand the underlying principle and to know why he does certain things.

The information contained in this little book is sufficient to enable the amateur sailor to take his boat anywhere, and is all that is used in ordinary practice at sea. It is hoped, however, that what he learns here will awaken in the reader a desire to pursue the study further,—in which case there is ample opportunity in the various interesting works that have been written on it.

Edmund T. Morton.

## CONTENTS

| CHAPTER | PAGE |
|---|---|
| I. Fundamental Terms | 11 |
| II. Time | 38 |
| III. The Sumner Line | 64 |
| IV. The Day's Work, Equal Altitude, and Ex-Meridian Sights | 85 |
| V. Star Sights | 98 |
| VI. Hints on Taking Observations | 120 |

# NAVIGATION FOR THE AMATEUR

# CHAPTER I

FUNDAMENTAL TERMS

THE branch of navigation used to determine a ships's position by observations of the heavenly bodies is called Nautical Astronomy. To be able to find one's position on the land or sea by observing any of the various bodies moving overhead gives one a better understanding of the order of the Universe than by merely reading a book about astronomy. By working out practical examples we are convinced beyond any doubt that we are poised on the surface of a ball flying through the immensity of space at terrific speed, as told us by astronomers. The opportunity for pursuing this interesting study is always at hand when we have leisure, while at sea a knowledge of it is of first importance in guiding ships across the ocean.

Take the Atlantic Coast chart from Cape Sable to Cape Hatteras, and you will find shown thereon the ragged coast line outlining

# AMATEUR NAVIGATION

the various harbors, bays, and sounds, and the lighthouses, lightships, fog signals, buoys, and soundings, all of which are necessary for pilot work in navigation. The margins of the chart are ruled off at the sides in degrees and minutes of latitude, and at the top and bottom in degrees and minutes of longitude. Straight parallel lines are drawn, connecting like degrees across the chart, dividing it into small rectangles from Lat. 35° North to Lat. 45° North, and from Long. 66° West to Long. 76° West.

Now, it will be seen at once, that when a vessel is beyond sight of the land and shore lights and on the deep waters of the Atlantic, the only method of plotting her position on the chart is by means of these lines of latitude and longitude.

Standing on the deck of a vessel with nothing in sight but the sea and the sky, it would seem an impossibility to determine one's position, except by calculating the courses and distances from the last point of departure. All that is needed, however, is a sextant, chronometer, Nautical Almanac, and a book of tables, and, of course, a clear horizon for taking altitudes of either sun, moon, planets or stars.

Mysterious as these calculations seem to a

## FUNDAMENTAL TERMS

novice, they are so simple that a schoolboy, knowing the common rules of arithmetic, can perform them correctly with a little practice. The real brain-work has been performed for us beforehand in the preparation of the data found in the Nautical Almanac and in the tables used.

To understand the whole science of navigation would require years of patient study and a high mathematical training, but sufficient knowledge to work an ordinary "noon sight" for latitude and "time sight" for longitude is soon acquired by proceeding according to the formulæ given. The beginner at first wonders if the vessel is really where the result of his observations put her. After proving one's position a few times, confidence is gained, and the results are taken as a matter of course.

Let us refer to our chart again and explain what these parallels of latitude and meridians of longitude mean. A notice on the chart reads,—" Mercator's Projection." From this we know that the chart before us represents that portion of the earth as a perfectly flat surface, distorted more and more as we proceed to the northern latitudes. Nevertheless, it is correct for all practical purposes in shaping

# AMATEUR NAVIGATION

courses, measuring distances, etc., if used intelligently. The degrees of longitude are made everywhere equal, while the degrees of latitude are lengthened toward the Poles. This needs an explanation.

Every circle is divided into 360 degrees, and the circumference of the earth at the Equator is divided into 360 degrees of 60 minutes each, and each minute is equal to one nautical mile. Now the meridians of longitude are imaginary circles running north and south over the earth's surface crossing the Equator at right angles. If these meridian circles are drawn through each degree at the Equator completely around the earth through both the North and South Poles, it will be seen that they all meet at a point at both poles. These meridians of longitude, sixty miles apart at the Equator, gradually approach each other until they meet at the poles, which shows how a degree of longitude is of different lengths, according to the latitude, or distance north or south of the Equator. A minute of longitude is equal to a nautical mile *only* at the Equator or near it.

The meridian circles are all equal, and on these can be measured the latitude or distance north or south of the Equator. Parallels of

## FUNDAMENTAL TERMS

latitude are small circles round the earth parallel to the Equator, the circles growing smaller with each degree north or south until the 90th degree is reached at the poles. In measuring latitude, we have both the Equator and Poles to measure from, definite and universal. In calculating the distance east and west, however, no such natural markings exist, and some definite line on the earth's surface must be established for this purpose. The meridian passing through Greenwich Observatory, England, is quite universally used in measuring longitude from 0° East to 180° and West to 180° in the circuit of the earth. The meridian of Greenwich is called the Prime Meridian.

The length of a degree of longitude can be measured between the meridians on any parallel of latitude desired. As before stated, these imaginary circles grow smaller as they approach the poles. The circumference of the earth at the Equator is a little less than 25,000 miles, one three-hundred-and-sixtieth of which is the length of one degree of longitude at the Equator. Thus, at the Equator 60 nautical miles constitute one degree of longitude; in latitude 21 degrees, 56 nautical miles make one degree of longitude; in latitude 60 degrees

## AMATEUR NAVIGATION

30 nautical miles make a degree of longitude, while at 90 degrees (the pole) the longitude is zero. Degrees of longitude of whatever length are divided into 60 minutes each. See Table No. 1 for the length of a degree of longi-

**LENGTHS, IN NAUTICAL MILES, OF A DEGREE OF LONGITUDE FOR EACH DEGREE OF LATITUDE FROM 0° TO 90°**

| Lat. Degrees | Miles | Lat. Degrees | Miles | Lat. Degrees | Miles |
|---|---|---|---|---|---|
| 1  | 59.99 | 31 | 51.43 | 61 | 29.09 |
| 2  | 59.96 | 32 | 50.88 | 62 | 28.17 |
| 3  | 59.92 | 33 | 50.32 | 63 | 27.74 |
| 4  | 59.85 | 34 | 49.74 | 64 | 26.30 |
| 5  | 59.77 | 35 | 49.15 | 65 | 25.36 |
| 6  | 59.67 | 36 | 48.54 | 66 | 24.40 |
| 7  | 59.55 | 37 | 47.92 | 67 | 23.44 |
| 8  | 59.42 | 38 | 47.28 | 68 | 22.48 |
| 9  | 59.26 | 39 | 46.63 | 69 | 21.50 |
| 10 | 59.09 | 40 | 45.96 | 70 | 20.52 |
| 11 | 58.89 | 41 | 45.28 | 71 | 19.53 |
| 12 | 58.69 | 42 | 44.59 | 72 | 18.54 |
| 13 | 58.46 | 43 | 43.88 | 73 | 17.54 |
| 14 | 58.22 | 44 | 43.16 | 74 | 16.54 |
| 15 | 57.95 | 45 | 42.43 | 75 | 15.53 |
| 16 | 57.67 | 46 | 41.68 | 76 | 14.52 |
| 17 | 57.38 | 47 | 40.92 | 77 | 13.50 |
| 18 | 57.06 | 48 | 40.15 | 78 | 12.48 |
| 19 | 56.73 | 49 | 39.36 | 79 | 11.45 |
| 20 | 56.38 | 50 | 38.57 | 80 | 10.42 |
| 21 | 56.01 | 51 | 37.76 | 81 | 9.38 |
| 22 | 55.63 | 52 | 36.94 | 82 | 8.35 |
| 23 | 55.23 | 53 | 36.11 | 83 | 7.31 |
| 24 | 54.81 | 54 | 35.27 | 84 | 6.27 |
| 25 | 54.38 | 55 | 34.41 | 85 | 5.23 |
| 26 | 53.93 | 56 | 33.45 | 86 | 4.18 |
| 27 | 53.46 | 57 | 32.68 | 87 | 3.14 |
| 28 | 52.97 | 58 | 31.79 | 88 | 2.00 |
| 29 | 52.48 | 59 | 30.09 | 89 | 1.05 |
| 30 | 51.96 | 60 | 30.00 | 90 | .00 |

Table I.

## FUNDAMENTAL TERMS

tude in nautical miles for each degree of latitude.

Degrees and minutes of latitude are everywhere equal, a minute being always equal to one nautical mile. According to exact measurements, there is a slight variation in different parts of the earth, but for our purpose it need not be further considered.

We now understand why the chart before us is not a true representation. The meridians, or lines running north and south, are drawn everywhere parallel instead of converging toward a point at the poles, as just explained. The degrees of longitude are here kept everywhere equal. To keep the right proportion between the degrees of latitude and longitude, the degrees of latitude are lengthened toward the poles. At the Equator the parallels of latitude and meridians of longitude form nearly exact squares, but gradually change proportion as they get farther and farther away from the Equator. When the 60th degree of latitude is reached the length of a degree of latitude will be twice as long as the degree of longitude. Fig. 1, Mercator's projection, from the Equator to 46 degrees north explains this point.

Much care must be exercised when measuring distances on the chart to apply the dividers

*AMATEUR NAVIGATION*

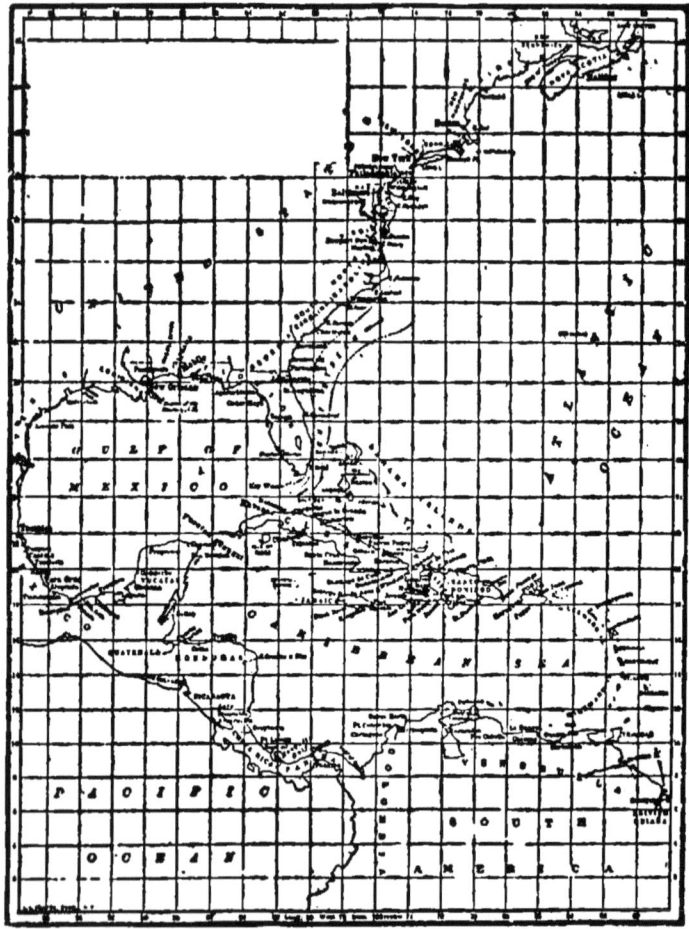

Fig. 1.—Mercator chart, showing how parallels of latitude are lengthened out as the poles are approached to maintain their proper proportion to the degrees of longitude, which on this projection are kept parallel.

to the degrees of latitude on the margin of the chart in the same latitude in which the vessel

## FUNDAMENTAL TERMS

is sailing. The same care must be used in measuring off minutes of latitude between degrees for plotting the vessel's position. Minutes of longitude can be taken anywhere on the top or bottom of the chart, as they are drawn everywhere the same; but cannot be used for measuring distances.

In finding the latitude by observation of a heavenly body, we need its meridian altitude; also, its declination or polar distance. We must understand these terms for our present use of them.

To an observer, the heavens look like an immense dome or vault, the stars and planets appearing like mere specks of light in the far distance. For the purpose of astronomical calculations, we must imagine a great circle described on the heavens in an east and west direction, dividing them into two equal parts, the same as the earth is divided into a northern and southern hemisphere by the Equator. This line would coincide exactly with the plane of the Equator of the earth if it was extended so as to cut the celestial sphere. This great circle is called the "Celestial Equator," and is everywhere 90° distant from the celestial poles. The "celestial poles" are imaginary points in

# AMATEUR NAVIGATION

the heavens directly in the zenith over the north and south poles of the earth.

The earth makes one revolution on its axis in twenty-four hours, and, as the circumference of the earth at the Equator is nearly 25,000 miles, a person sitated at the Equator must be traveling in an easterly direction over 1,000 miles an hour. A person at the exact pole of the earth would have no daily motion. This illustrates how the stars appear to rise above the eastern horizon each night, describe exact parallel circles through the heavens, and set again below the western horizon. Stars near the Celestial Equator appear to move very rapidly, while those near the poles seem to have very little motion. For instance, the North Star is slightly over one degree from the celestial pole, and it describes a minute circle around this imaginary point daily. To a casual observer, it remains at a fixed point.

These heavenly bodies have their latitude and longitude in the sky, giving each its definite position in relation to the others, much the same as places are defined on the surface of the earth. The angular distance of sun, moon, or stars north or south of the Celestial Equator is called the declination of that body, reckoned

## FUNDAMENTAL TERMS

in degrees and minutes of arc. The angular distance of the body observed from the celestial pole is called the Polar Distance. If the observer is in north latitude, and the declination of the body observed is north, the sum of the declination and polar distance will, of course, be 90°. If, however, the observer's latitude

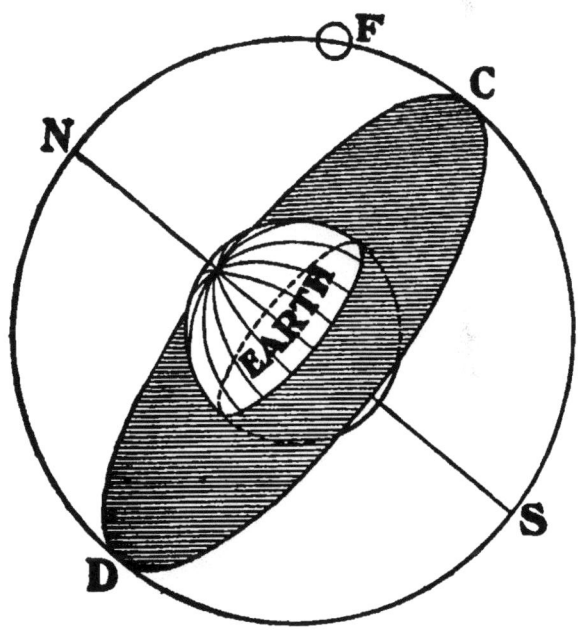

Fig. 2.—N and S, Celestial Poles; C D, Celestial Equator (plane of earth's equator extended to cut the celestial sphere); N C S D, Celestial sphere; F, Position of Sun; Arc N F = polar distance; Arc C F = declination.

# AMATEUR NAVIGATION

is north and the declination is south, the polar distance will be 90° plus the declination. If in south latitude, the polar distance would be reckoned from the south pole in a similar manner. (See Fig. 2.)

The meridian of any place is an imaginary arc of a circle passing through the zenith in an exact north and south direction, cutting the horizon at the north and south points. When the sun or other body crosses this line it is said to be " on meridian." The body has then reached its highest altitude, and, after passing the meridian, the altitude grows less, until it finally reaches the western horizon.

### Latitude

The latitude of a place is its distance north or south of the Equator, and the simplest method of finding it at sea is by taking a meridian altitude of the sun.

The latitude may be found by a meridian altitude of any heavenly body whose declination is known, and by ex-meridian altitudes under favorable conditions.

The angular distance from the zenith to the Celestial Equator is always equal to the

## FUNDAMENTAL TERMS

distance of the observer from the Equator of the earth, which is the latitude.

The problem, therefore, is to find the distance of the sun from the zenith when it is on meridian and apply to it the distance of the sun from the Celestial Equator, called its declination.

Now, it can be easily understood how an observer's position north or south of the Equator can be found when the meridian altitude and declination of a heavenly body are known. The sun is used for this purpose more than any other body, and will serve best in further explanation.

If the meridian altitude of the sun is 90° (or directly overhead), and it has no declination, the observer must be on the Equator. If the meridian altitude of the sun is 90° and its declination is 10° North, then the latitude must be 10° North. The sun's declination varies from 23° 27′ North about June 22 each year to 23° 27′ South about December 22. The correct declination for each day of the year is calculated and published in the Nautical Almanac for the especial use of navigators, so that all one requires is the meridian altitude of the sun at noon, and by working out a simple formula, the latitude is known. The

## AMATEUR NAVIGATION

latitude found in this way can always be relied upon as being correct.

The arc of the meridian from the horizon to the zenith measures 90°. The altitude of a body subtracted from 90° will give its zenith distance.

The formula then is as follows: Observe a meridian altitude of the sun and correct it for semi-diameter, refraction, dip of the horizon and parallax. Subtract the corrected altitude from 90° to get the zenith distance. If the sun bears south, name the zenith distance north; but if the sun bears north, name the zenith distance south. Now take the sun's corrected declination from the Nautical Almanac for that date and mark it north or south, as it is found there. If the sun's declination and zenith distance are both named north or both named south, their sum will be the latitude, of that name. But if one is found to be north and the other south, their difference will be the latitude, to be named after the *greater* of the two quantities.

Here is an example:

# FUNDAMENTAL TERMS

June 18, 1910.  Sun's corrected altitude.. 79° 49' 31" S.
                                           90° 00' 00"

Zenith distance ........................ 10° 10' 29" N.
Corrected declination                    23° 24' 21" N.

Latitude at noon ........................33° 34' 50" N.

After a little practical experience in working out the latitude in this way the rule will hardly be given a thought.  The navigator will know approximately his position—that is, within a degree—and the result will show at once whether the zenith distance and declination have been applied correctly.  However, this is not always so evident when the ship changes the bearing of the sun from north to south, or vice versa, as often occurs when sailing in the tropics.

## THE SEXTANT

The observed altitude is the angular distance of a heavenly body above the visible horizon as measured with a sextant in ordinary practice at sea.  The sextant is a light, portable instrument invented for use in measuring angles, and especially designed for use on shipboard where fixed instruments cannot be employed.  Next to the compass it is used more than any other instrument in navigation.

## AMATEUR NAVIGATION

Fig. 3 shows this instrument with all its essential parts.

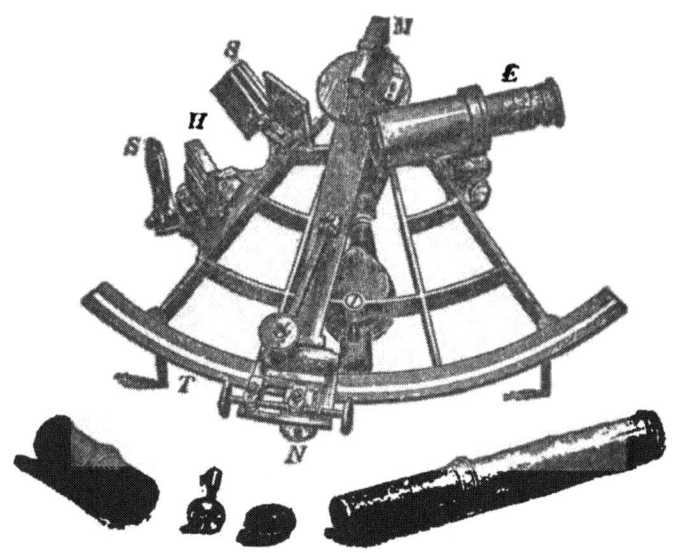

Fig. 3.—The Sextant. M, Index Mirror; M N, Index Arm, pivoted in center of arc; T, Tangent Screw; H, Horizon Glass, the lower half being silvered, the upper half transparent; E, Eye Glass or Telescope; S, Colored Shade Glasses to protect the eyes from the sun; S', Colored Glass for use when the sun is at a low altitude. A vernier is carried on the index arm,

The arc consists of about one-sixth of a circle, as its name indicates, and is usually made of silver. This arc is divided into half degrees, which are named as whole degrees. Altitudes over 120° can be measured with it, but it is seldom an altitude is taken at sea over 90°. These degrees on the arc are divided

## FUNDAMENTAL TERMS

into six parts of 10 minutes each. A graduated scale on the vernier further divides the reading to 10 seconds, though the scale varies on different instruments. The colored shade glasses of red and green are used to subdue the light and protect the eyes from the brilliancy of the sun. Those placed below the horizon glass are only needed when the sun is at a low altitude, making a glare upon the surface of the water between the observer and the horizon.

When ready to use, the observer holds the sextant with his right hand by the wooden handle at the back, and, facing the sun, looks through the telescope and horizon-glass toward the horizon. Then the vernier is moved forward along the arc by the left hand until the reflected image of the sun, passing from the index mirror ($M$ in Fig. 4) and again reflected in the silvered part of the horizon-glass (H), is seen to touch its lower edge (or limb, as it is called) on the horizon. When the sun is brought nearly in contact with the horizon the vernier may be clamped to the arc by the screw on the under side. The contact is then made with great precision by moving the tangent screw ($T$, Fig. 3) found on the forward part of the vernier.

# AMATEUR NAVIGATION

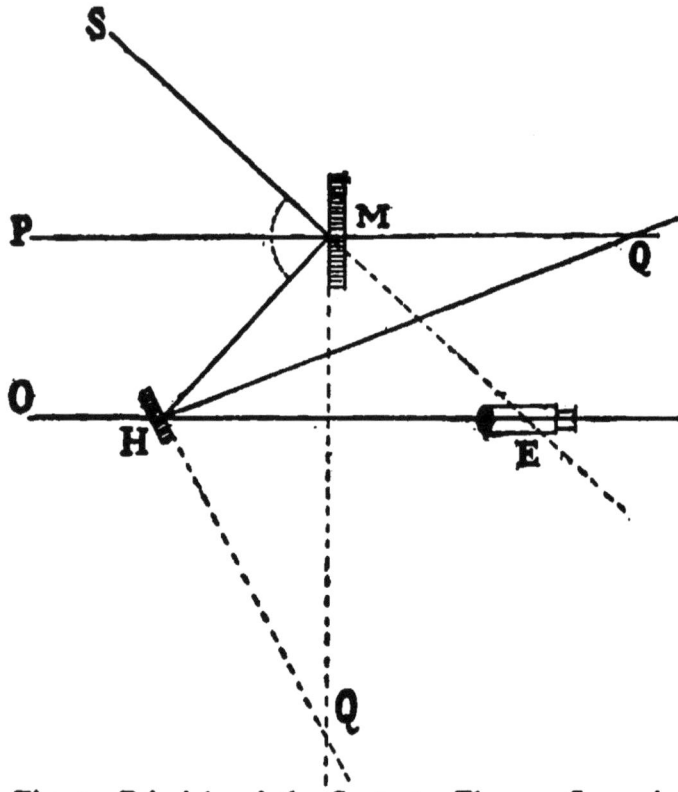

Fig. 4.—Principle of the Sextant. The ray S, coming from the sun, is reflected on index glass M, and then at horizon glass H, and is made to coincide with the ray O H coming from the horizon and seen through the eye glass E.

The reading on the arc where the arrow on the vernier cuts it will be the sun's observed altitude. If the mark on the vernier does not coincide exactly with a division of the scale on the arc, take the reading from the nearest mark to the *right* of it. Then look along the

# FUNDAMENTAL TERMS

graduated scale and see where the divisions on the two scales exactly coincide. Take these odd minutes and add them to the first reading on the arc for the altitude. The time by chronometer may be taken at the instant of contact, if desired.

### OBSERVED ALTITUDE AND CORRECTIONS

The observer should begin his observation for meridian altitude ten or fifteen minutes before noon, and carefully watch the sun as it rises to obtain its highest altitude at culmination, which will be 12 o'clock, noon, local apparent time at ship. The sun will then bear due north or due south, according to one's position.

The observed altitude must be corrected, for various causes, to obtain the true altitude. The corrections to be made are for index error (if any), semi-diameter, dip of the horizon, refraction, and parallax. The meaning of these terms follow: Index error refers to any error known to exist in the sextant used.

### SEMI-DIAMETER, DIP, REFRACTION, PARALLAX

As the sun's lower limb is observed, the semi-

# AMATEUR NAVIGATION

diameter, or half the altitude of the diameter of the sun, must be added to get the altitude of its center. The sun's semi-diameter is greatest in December, when the earth is nearest to the sun, it then being 16′ 18″, while it is the least in June, when the earth is farthest from the sun, it then being 15′ 45″. However, 16 minutes is near enough to be used for all practical purposes. The sun's semi-diameter is given for noon each day in the Nautical Almanac.

The tables, hereafter referred to, are to be found in Bowditch's Epitome of Navigation. The dip of the horizon is the angular difference between the true horizon and the horizon as seen by an observer, and the amount depends upon the height of the observer's eye above the level of the sea. It is clearly shown in Fig. 5.

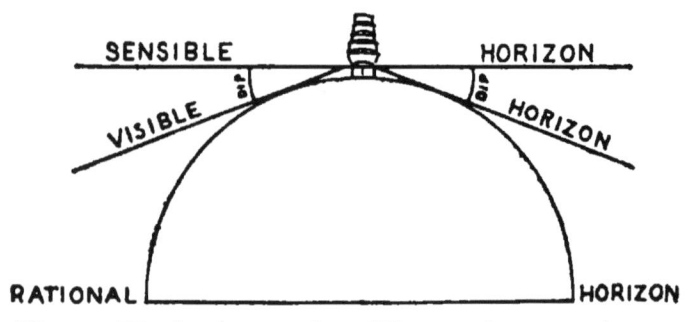

Fig. 5.—Dip is the angular difference between the true horizon and the horizon as seen by an observer.

## FUNDAMENTAL TERMS

This correction, found in Table No. 14, is always to be subtracted from the observed altitude.

Refraction is the downward deflection of a ray of light entering the atmosphere of the earth, causing a celestial body to appear higher than it actually is. Refraction changes as the condition of the atmosphere changes, as shown by the thermometer and barometer.

It is greatest when the observed body is near the horizon, as, with the sun or moon near rising or setting, refraction amounts to two-thirds of a degree. This is more than the diameter of either body, which is about one-half a degree. Refraction grows less as the altitude increases. Table No. 20 gives the correction of the sun's apparent altitude for refraction and parallax. This correction is always to be subtracted from the altitude.

Parallax is the difference between the direction of a body as actually observed and what it would be if seen from the center of the earth. Except with the moon, parallax is of little consequence in ordinary practice at sea, and the correction for it is usually omitted. If used, it is always added to the altitude, being greatest when the observed object is near the

# *AMATEUR NAVIGATION*

horizon and disappearing when the body is near the zenith.

These corrections may each be applied separately to the observed altitude, but a simpler method is to subtract the corrections for refraction and dip of the horizon from the semi-diameter and add the result to the observed altitude. Take the example given before to see how this works out:

```
    June 18, 1910.
Semi-diameter from Nautical Almanac .....    + 15' 46"
Refraction and par. for 79°, Table 20—     9"
Dip of horizon, height 10 ft., Table 14—3' 06"
                                         ————
                                         —3' 15"       3' 15"
                                                      ————
To be added to observed altitude............         12' 31"
Observed meridian altitude................   79° 37' 00"
                                              ——————————
True central altitude                         79° 49' 31"
                                              90° 00' 00"
                                              ——————————
Zenith distance ..........................    10° 10' 29"
Sun's corrected declination from N. A........ 23° 24' 21"
                                              ——————————
Latitude at noon .........................    33° 34' 50"
   (See Fig. 6 for declination and corrections)
```

Here is an example where the latitude is north and the declination south. On January 1, 1911, the meridian altitude of the sun was 38° 02' bearing South. Approximate longitude 74° 00' West. Height of the eye, 10 feet.

## FUNDAMENTAL TERMS

| | |
|---|---|
| Semi-diameter from N. A............ | + 16′ 18″ |
| Dip of horizon, Table No. 14.......... | − 3′ 06″ |
| Refraction and parallax, Table No. 20 B | − 1′ 08″ |
| Correction to be added............... | 12′ 04″ |
| Observed meridian altitude............ | 38° 02′ 00″ |
| True central altitude................ | 38° 14′ 04″ |
| | 90° 00′ 00″ |
| Zenith distance...................... | 51° 45′ 56″ North |
| Corrected declination from N. A...... | 23° 05′ 36″ South |
| Latitude at noon.................... | 28° 40′ 20″ North |

Here is an example in south latitude. On October 10, 1910, the meridian altitude of the sun was 61° 30′ bearing North. Approximate longitude, 45° West. Height of the eye, 18 feet.

| | |
|---|---|
| Semi-diameter from N. A. ........ | + 16′ 03″ |
| Dip of horizon for 18 feet........ | −4′ 09″ |
| Refraction and parallax, Table 20 B.. | −0′ 28″ |
| Correction to be added ............. | 11′ 26″ |
| Observed altitude ................... | 61° 30′ 00″ North |
| | 61° 41′ 26″ North |
| | 90° 00′ 00″ |
| Zenith distance | 28° 18′ 34″ South |
| Declination from N. A. ........ 6° 24′ 41″ | |
| Cor. Long. 45° W. = 3 hrs        +2′ 51″ | |
| Declination | 6° 27′ 32″ South |
| Latitude     ....................... | 34° 46′ 06″ South |

| | | AT GREENWICH MEAN NOON. | | | | | | |
|---|---|---|---|---|---|---|---|---|
| Day of Month | Day of Week | THE SUN'S | | | | Equation of Time, to be Added to Subtracted from Mean Time | | Sidereal Time at Right Ascension of Mean Sun |
| | | Apparent Right Ascension | Diff. for 1 Hour | Apparent Declination | Diff. for 1 Hour | | Diff. for 1 Hour | |
| | | h. m. s. | s. | ° ' " | " | m. s. | s. | h. m. s. |
| Wed. | 1 | 4 33 50.49 | 10.221 | N.21 58 30.3 | +20.90 | 2 31.02 | 0.365 | 4 36 21.51 |
| Thur. | 2 | 4 37 56.01 | 10.239 | 22 6 42.9 | 20.04 | 2 22.05 | 0.382 | 4 40 18.06 |
| Frid. | 3 | 4 42 1.95 | 10.256 | 22 14 32.4 | 19.07 | 2 12.66 | 0.399 | 4 44 14.62 |
| Sat. | 4 | 4 46 8.29 | 10.272 | 22 21 58.7 | +18.10 | 2 2.88 | 0.415 | 4 48 11.18 |
| SUN. | 5 | 4 50 15.01 | 10.287 | 22 29 1.6 | 17.12 | 1 52.73 | 0.430 | 4 52 7.74 |
| Mon. | 6 | 4 54 22.08 | 10.301 | 22 35 41.0 | 16.14 | 1 42.22 | 0.445 | 4 56 4.30 |
| Tues. | 7 | 4 58 29.48 | 10.314 | 22 41 56.7 | +15.19 | 1 31.38 | 0.458 | 5 0 0.85 |
| Wed. | 8 | 5 2 37.18 | 10.327 | 22 47 48.4 | 14.25 | 1 20.23 | 0.470 | 5 3 57.41 |
| Thur. | 9 | 5 6 45.16 | 10.338 | 22 53 16.0 | 13.24 | 1 8.80 | 0.481 | 5 7 53.96 |
| Frid. | 10 | 5 10 53.40 | 10.349 | 22 58 19.5 | +12.13 | 0 57.12 | 0.491 | 5 11 50.52 |
| Sat. | 11 | 5 15 1.87 | 10.358 | 23 2 58.7 | 11.12 | 0 45.21 | 0.500 | 5 15 47.08 |
| SUN. | 12 | 5 19 10.54 | 10.367 | 23 7 13.6 | 10.20 | 0 33.10 | 0.508 | 5 19 43.64 |
| Mon. | 13 | 5 23 19.39 | 10.374 | 23 11 4.1 | + 9.08 | 0 20.81 | 0.515 | 5 23 40.20 |
| Tues. | 14 | 5 27 28.40 | 10.380 | 23 14 30.0 | 8.05 | 0 8.36 | 0.521 | 5 27 36.76 |
| Wed. | 15 | 5 31 37.54 | 10.385 | 23 17 31.2 | 7.02 | 0 4.22 | 0.526 | 5 31 33.32 |
| Thur. | 16 | 5 35 46.80 | 10.389 | 23 20 7.7 | + 6.00 | 0 16.92 | 0.531 | 5 35 29.88 |
| Frid. | 17 | 5 39 56.15 | 10.391 | 23 22 19.5 | 4.97 | 0 29.72 | 0.534 | 5 39 26.43 |
| Sat. | 18 | 5 44 5.57 | 10.393 | 23 24 6.6 | 3.94 | 0 42.58 | 0.537 | 5 43 22.99 |
| SUN. | 19 | 5 48 15.04 | 10.396 | 23 25 28.9 | + 2.91 | 0 55.40 | 0.538 | 5 47 19.55 |
| Mon. | 20 | 5 52 24.54 | 10.396 | 23 26 26.4 | 1.87 | 1 8.43 | 0.539 | 5 51 16.11 |
| Tues. | 21 | 5 56 34.05 | 10.396 | 23 26 59.2 | + 0.84 | 1 21.38 | 0.539 | 5 55 12.67 |
| Wed. | 22 | 6 0 43.54 | 10.395 | 23 27 7.2 | - 0.19 | 1 34.32 | 0.538 | 5 59 9.22 |
| Thur. | 23 | 6 4 52.99 | 10.393 | 23 26 50.4 | 1.22 | 1 47.21 | 0.536 | 6 3 5.78 |
| Frid. | 24 | 6 9 2.39 | 10.390 | 23 26 8.8 | 2.25 | 2 0.05 | 0.533 | 6 7 2.34 |
| Sat. | 25 | 6 13 11.72 | 10.387 | 23 25 2.5 | - 3.28 | 2 12.82 | 0.529 | 6 10 58.90 |
| SUN. | 26 | 6 17 20.93 | 10.382 | 23 23 31.5 | 4.31 | 2 25.49 | 0.525 | 6 14 55.46 |
| Mon. | 27 | 6 21 30.06 | 10.377 | 23 21 35.9 | 5.34 | 2 38.05 | 0.520 | 6 18 52.02 |
| Tues. | 28 | 6 25 39.05 | 10.371 | 23 19 15.7 | - 6.36 | 2 50.48 | 0.515 | 6 22 48.57 |
| Wed. | 29 | 6 29 47.90 | 10.365 | 23 16 30.9 | 7.39 | 3 2.77 | 0.508 | 6 26 45.13 |
| Thur. | 30 | 6 33 56.57 | 10.357 | 23 13 21.7 | 8.40 | 3 14.88 | 0.500 | 6 30 41.69 |
| Frid. | 31 | 6 38 5.04 | 10.349 | N.23 9 48.0 | - 9.41 | 3 26.80 | 0.492 | 6 34 38.24 |

NOTE.—The semidiameter for noon may be assumed the same as that for apparent noon. The sign + prefixed to the hourly change of declination indicates that north declinations are increasing, the sign — indicates that north declinations are decreasing.

Diff. for 1 Hour. + 9¹.8563 (Table III.)

Fig. 6.—Page from the Nautical Almanac, showing declination for the month of June, 1910. In the first example given the declination for the 18th is taken for Greenwich mean noon, to which is added the difference for five hours, as the ship's position, approximately 75° West, is five hours later than Greenwich noon, the declination being on the increase and the hourly difference being shown in the adjoining column.

# FUNDAMENTAL TERMS

| Day of week | Day of month | AT GREENWICH APPARENT NOON. ||||||| |
|---|---|---|---|---|---|---|---|---|
| | | THE SUN'S |||||| Sidereal Time of Semi-diameter Passing Meridian | Equation of Time, to be Subtracted from Added to Apparent Time | Diff. for 1 Hour |
| | | Apparent Right Ascension | Diff. for 1 Hour | Apparent Declination | Diff. for 1 Hour | Semi-diameter | | | |
| | | h. m. s. | s. | ° ′ ″ | ″ | ′ ″ | m. s. | m. s. | s. |
| Wed. | 1 | 4 33 50.08 | 10.222 | N.21 58 29.4 | +20.99 | 15 48.02 | 68.34 | 2 31.02 | 0.365 |
| Thur. | 2 | 4 37 55.62 | 10.239 | 22 6 42.1 | 20.04 | 15 47.87 | 68.40 | 2 22.06 | 0.382 |
| Frid. | 3 | 4 42 1.58 | 10.256 | 22 14 31.8 | 19.07 | 15 47.73 | 68.46 | 2 12.67 | 0.399 |
| Sat. | 4 | 4 46 7.95 | 10.272 | 22 21 58.2 | +18.10 | 15 47.59 | 68.51 | 2 2.88 | 0.415 |
| SUN. | 5 | 4 50 14.70 | 10.287 | 22 29 1.1 | 17.12 | 15 47.46 | 68.56 | 1 52.73 | 0.430 |
| Mon. | 6 | 4 54 21.80 | 10.301 | 22 35 40.5 | 16.14 | 15 47.34 | 68.60 | 1 42.23 | 0.443 |
| Tues. | 7 | 4 58 29.23 | 10.314 | 22 41 56.2 | +15.15 | 15 47.22 | 68.65 | 1 31.38 | 0.458 |
| Wed. | 8 | 5 2 36.96 | 10.327 | 22 47 48.1 | 14.15 | 15 47.11 | 68.69 | 1 20.22 | 0.470 |
| Thur. | 9 | 5 6 44.97 | 10.338 | 22 53 15.9 | 13.14 | 15 47.00 | 68.73 | 1 8.79 | 0.481 |
| Frid. | 10 | 5 10 53.24 | 10.349 | 22 58 19.4 | +12.13 | 15 46.90 | 68.76 | 0 57.11 | 0.491 |
| Sat. | 11 | 5 15 1.74 | 10.358 | 23 2 58.6 | 11.11 | 15 46.80 | 68 79 | 0 45.21 | 0.500 |
| SUN. | 12 | 5 19 10.45 | 10.367 | 23 7 13.5 | 10.10 | 15 46.72 | 68.82 | 0 33.10 | 0.508 |
| Mon. | 13 | 5 23 19.34 | 10.374 | 23 11 4.1 | + 9.08 | 15 46.62 | 68.85 | 0 20.80 | 0.515 |
| Tues. | 14 | 5 27 28.38 | 10.380 | 23 14 30.0 | 8.05 | 15 46 54 | 68 87 | 0 8.35 | 0.521 |
| Wed. | 15 | 5 31 37.56 | 10.385 | 23 17 31.2 | 7.02 | 15 46.46 | 68.89 | 0 + 4.23 | 0.526 |
| Thur. | 16 | 5 35 46.85 | 10.389 | 23 20 7.7 | + 6.00 | 15 46 38 | 68.91 | 0 16.93 | 0.531 |
| Frid. | 17 | 5 39 56.24 | 10.392 | 23 22 19.6 | 4.97 | 15 46.31 | 68.92 | 0 29.73 | 0.534 |
| Sat. | 18 | 5 44 5.70 | 10.395 | 23 24 .6.7 | 3.94 | 15 46.24 | 68.93 | 0 42.60 | 0.537 |
| SUN. | 19 | 5 48 15.21 | 10.396 | 23 25 28.9 | + 2.91 | 15 46.18 | 68.94 | 0 55.51 | 0.538 |
| Mon. | 20 | 5 52 24.75 | 10.396 | 23 26 26.4 | 1.87 | 15 46.12 | 68.94 | 1 8.45 | 0.539 |
| Tues. | 21 | 5 56 34.29 | 10.396 | 23 26 59.2 | + 0.84 | 15 46.07 | 68.95 | 1 21.39 | 0.539 |
| Wed. | 22 | 6 0 43.82 | 10.395 | 23 27 7.2 | - 0.19 | 15 46.02 | 68.95 | 1 34.32 | 0.538 |
| Thur. | 23 | 6 4 53.31 | 10.393 | 23 26 50.4 | 1.22 | 15 45.97 | 68.94 | 1 47.22 | 0.536 |
| Frid. | 24 | 6 9 2.75 | 10.390 | 23 26 8.8 | 2.25 | 15 45.92 | 68.93 | 2 0.07 | 0.533 |
| Sat. | 25 | 6 13 12.11 | 10.387 | 23 25 2.4 | - 3.28 | 15 45.88 | 68.92 | 2 12.84 | 0.529 |
| SUN. | 26 | 6 17 21.38 | 10.381 | 23 23 31.4 | 4.31 | 15 45.84 | 68.90 | 2 25.52 | 0.525 |
| Mon. | 27 | 6 21 30.53 | 10.377 | 23 21 35.7 | 5.34 | 15 45.80 | 68.88 | 2 38.09 | 0.520 |
| Tues. | 28 | 6 25 39.55 | 10.371 | 23 19 15.4 | - 6.36 | 15 45.76 | 68.86 | 2 50.52 | 0.515 |
| Wed. | 29 | 6 29 48.43 | 10.365 | 23 16 30.5 | 7.39 | 15 45.73 | 68.83 | 3 2.80 | 0.508 |
| Thur. | 30 | 6 33 57.14 | 10.357 | 23 13 21.2 | 8.40 | 15 45.71 | 68.80 | 3 14.92 | 0.500 |
| Frid. | 31 | 6 38 5.64 | 10.349 | N.23 9 47.5 | - 9.41 | 15 45.69 | 68.76 | 3 26.85 | 0.491 |

NOTE.—The mean time of semidiameter passing the meridian may be found by subtracting s.15 from the sidereal data. The sign + prefixed to the hourly change of declination indicates that north declinations are increasing, the sign — indicates that north declinations are decreasing.

Fig. 6a.—Page from Nautical Almanac using Greenwich apparent time instead of mean time.

# AMATEUR NAVIGATION

The navigator in daily practice finds this correction nearly constant; so, instead of adding the correction to the altitude, he subtracts it from 90°, thus: 90° — 12′ = 89° 48′. Then he can at once subtract his observed altitude from 89° 48′, which gives him the zenith distance: 89° 48′

Observed altitude .......................... 79° 37′

Zenith distance ............................ 10° 11′ N.
Declination .... ............................ 23° 24′ N.

Latitude .......... ........................ 33° 35′ N.

Some have objected to teaching the use of the constants 89° 48′ or 89° 50′ in this way, yet it is the method almost universally used among practical navigators.

Another constant may be prepared that is accurate, to which the observed meridian altitude may be applied at once in the following manner: Instead of adding or subtracting the declination from the remainder, apply it to 90° at once in the same way and subtract the altitude correction from this sum. To this constant now ready may be applied the altitude as soon as taken.

Take the former example and use it in this way:

## *FUNDAMENTAL TERMS*

|  |  |
|---|---|
| | 90° 00′ 00″ |
| Declination .... .................. | 23° 24′ 21″ N. |
| | 113° 24′ 21″ |
| Corrections .... ................ | 12′ 31″ |
| Constant ........ ..................... | 113° 11′ 50″ |
| Observed altitude .................. | 79° 37′ 00″ |
| Latitude ............ ............... | 33° 34′ 50″ N. |

The former method seems preferable, whereby the zenith distance is found and applied to the declination according to the rule. It is clearer to one's mind in doing the work, the principle involved being the same as employed on every ship.

# CHAPTER II

### TIME

TIME is defined as a portion of duration, and as it is measured by different periods and measurements we must understand the kinds of time used by navigators.

The ordinary civil time of every day use is measured by the daily revolution of the sun, and, commencing at midnight, counts 12 hours A. M. and 12 hours P. M.

Astronomical time begins at noon and counts through 24 hours to the next noon, keeping the same date, that is, changing the date at noon instead of at the midnight previous, as in civil time. Thus, 8 A. M., Jan. 16th., civil time would be 20 hours Jan. 15th astronomical time. From noon until midnight the hours would be numbered the same by both times, Astronomical time would continue after midnight, numbering the hours 13 and 14 to 24 hours under the date of the previous day. This must be borne in mind when using the Nautical Almanac.

## *TIME*

Apparent time is time by the sun as shown by a sun dial, it being noon on each day at the time the sun crosses the meridian of any place. Everywhere north and south on this meridian it will be noon at the same time. This time makes the days of unequal length, owing to the variation in the time of the sun crossing the meridian, caused by the obliquity of the Ecliptic with the Equator and the difference in velocity of movement at those times when the sun is nearest the earth and when it is farthest away.

Mean time is also solar time, but so divided that every day is of equal length throughout the year, such as would be shown by a perfect running watch or chronometer.

Sidereal time marks the time by the stars instead of the sun, and will be explained in connection with star observations.

### The Chronometer.

The chronometer is a finely constructed watch or clock made for keeping time with great exactness and compensated for changes in temperature, to which it is especially liable when at sea. It is set in gimbals, as is a compass, so as always to lie horizontally in spite of the pitch-

## AMATEUR NAVIGATION

ing and rolling of the vessel. When taken on board ship it is placed in a thickly padded box as a protection against sudden jolts and vibrations. It should be kept in a room with an even temperature if possible, and should not be opened and shut except when necessary to use it.

The key-hole is on the under side and the instrument must be inverted to wind it. This hole is covered by a brass plate arranged with a spring so as to move back over the hole when the key is removed. This guards its delicate parts from dust, moisture, and sudden changes of temperature. The box when placed on board ship should be firmly fastened with screws in a safe and convenient place for use, where good light will illumine its face day and night.

Most chronometers will run for 56 hours, but should nevertheless be wound daily at the same time and with the same even movement in winding. As they will run 56 hours they do not run down however, through failure to wind at the regular time. The second hand, beating half-seconds, is near the bottom of the face, while near the top is another hand moving on a dial marked from 0 to 56 hours to show how

## *TIME*

many hours it has been running since being wound. As chronometers may change their rate of loss or gain when a ship is under way, this rate can be calculated at the end of each voyage, when ships return frequently to the same port.

Vessels should carry either one chronometer, or three, as if two are carried and any difference is found between them, it is only a source of confusion. When two agree and the other differs, the latter is supposed to be in error. In taking daily observations at sea, a good running watch may be used to advantage, if frequent comparisons are made with the chronometer to prevent or detect any errors.

### Equation of Time

The method of finding the longitude is merely to find the exact time at one's position and the exact time at Greenwich at the same instant, and to turn the difference of time into degrees and minutes of longitude. For this purpose a chronometer is needed regulated to Greenwich mean time, with its error and daily rate of gaining or losing. When a chronometer is taken from a nau-

## AMATEUR NAVIGATION

tical store a slip of paper is given with it, upon which is stated its error on a given date and its daily rate of gaining or losing, as the case may be. The error can then be reckoned for each day and set down in the Nautical Almanac for a month in advance, if desired, ready for daily use.

The time by chronometer is Greenwich Mean Time, while the time found by observation of the sun is Apparent Time. The difference between mean time and apparent time is called the Equation of Time, which is given for each day of the year in the Nautical Almanac.

An apparent solar day is the interval of time between two successive transits of the sun over the same meridian. As such intervals of time make the days of slightly unequal length, a fictitious time has been invented, called mean solar time, which makes all the days of the year of equal length. This is done for the purpose of regulating clocks and chronometers to a uniform rate instead of changing the time each noon as the sun crosses the meridian. Four times during a year mean time and apparent time are the same. At other times the mean time is either before or behind apparent time, the greatest difference amounting to over six-

## TIME

teen minutes. This difference is called the Equation of Time, before mentioned, and the apparent time may be changed to mean time, or the Greenwich mean time may be changed to apparent time by applying the Equation of Time as indicated in the Nautical Almanac. Both times must be of mean time or both of apparent time before their difference is taken to get the longitude.

Both the Equation of Time and the declination of the sun are given in the Almanac for Greenwich noon. As these quantities are changing daily, the hourly differences are given in an adjoining column, and they must be corrected to time of observation, according as that time is before or after Greenwich noon. The correction must be added or subtracted as the quantity is shown to be *increasing* or *decreasing* daily. See Figs. 6 and 6a, pages from Nautical Almanac.

The following table gives the times of agreement and greatest differences for the year 1911:

Feb. 12., Sun. 14m 25s slow
April 16, Sun. 0  0
May 15th, Sun. 3m 49s fast
June 15th, Sun. 0m 0

July 27, Sun. 6m 20s slow
June 15th, Sun. 0  0
Nov. 4. Sun...16m 21s fast
Dec 25th, Sun.. 0  0

# *AMATEUR NAVIGATION.*

### Finding the Longitude

As the sun appears to make one revolution around the earth in a day (that is, 360 degrees in 24 hours), apparently it moves to the westward 15 degrees each hour. At a place 15° west of Greenwich the sun will rise one hour later than at Greenwich, and at a place 15° east of Greenwich the sun will rise one hour earlier than at Greenwich, and so on. In comparing the time between two meridians the time at the most easterly meridian will be the greatest or latest. At 12 o'clock Greenwich noon it will be only 7 A. M. in Longitude 75° West, just five hours earlier. The problem, therefore, is to find the correct local time at a given instant

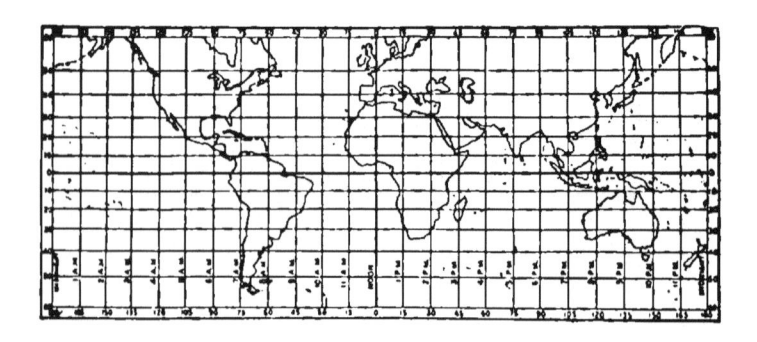

Fig. 7.—Chart showing local time for each 15 degrees of longitude when it is mean noon at Greenwich.

## TIME

and apply it to the Greenwich time taken from the chronometer at the same instant. Fig. 7 is a chart showing this plainly.

We have seen that a meridian altitude is the best for latitude; but for longitude, observations of the sun taken about 8 A. M. or 4 P. M. are the best, as the altitude is then changing rapidly, and, consequently, the time can be determined more accurately. Whenever practicable, the morning or afternoon sights should be taken when the sun is on or near the prime vertical—that is, when it is bearing due east or due west—as then even a large error in the latitude used will make only slight difference in the longitude obtained. An altitude of at least 20° is preferred, to prevent great errors by refraction.

To find the longitude, take an altitude of the sun with the sextant at the most favorable time in the forenoon or afternoon, and at the instant the sun's lower limb is brought in contact with the horizon note the exact time by chronometer. Correct the chronometer time for its error (if slow, add; if fast, subtract the error), which will give the correct Greenwich mean time. Correct the altitude observed for instrumental error, semi-diameter, refraction,

## AMATEUR NAVIGATION

and dip of the horizon. This will give the sun's true central altitude.

Then find the latitude by account at time of observation. The latitude is usually found at noon by a meridian altitude of the sun. If the time sight is taken in the morning the latitude is brought back from noon; or if in the afternoon, it is carried forward to time of observation by applying the difference of latitude made during the interval. To do this, take the time, compass course, and distance sailed in the interval from noon to time of sight and inspect Table No. 1, Bowditch. The course will be found at either the top or bottom of the page. Then find the distance in the column so marked above or below where the course is found. Three columns are found here, marked distance, latitude, and departure, the departure being the distance in nautical miles made east or west. If the course is found at the top of the page, the difference of latitude must be taken from column marked latitude at the top. If course is found at bottom of the page, it must be taken from column marked latitude at bottom of page. To the latitude found at noon add or subtract the difference of latitude found in this table, which will give the approximate

Page 208] TABLE 1.

Difference of Latitude and Departure for 2 Points.

| N.N.E. | | | N.N.W. | | | S.S.E. | | | S.S.W. | | | | | |
|---|---|---|---|---|---|---|---|---|---|---|---|---|---|---|
| Dist. | Lat. | Dep. | Dist. | Lat. | Dep. | Dist. | Lat. | Dep. | Dist. | Lat. | Dep. | Dist. | Lat. | Dep. |
| 1 | 0.9 | 0.4 | 61 | 56.4 | 23.3 | 121 | 111.8 | 46.3 | 181 | 167.2 | 69.3 | 241 | 222.7 | 92.2 |
| 2 | 1.8 | 0.8 | 62 | 57.3 | 23.7 | 22 | 112.7 | 46.7 | 82 | 168.1 | 69.6 | 42 | 223.6 | 92.6 |
| 3 | 2.8 | 1.1 | 63 | 58.2 | 24.1 | 23 | 113.6 | 47.1 | 83 | 169.1 | 70.0 | 43 | 224.5 | 93.0 |
| 4 | 3.7 | 1.5 | 64 | 59.1 | 24.5 | 24 | 114.6 | 47.5 | 84 | 170.0 | 70.4 | 44 | 225.4 | 93.4 |
| 5 | 4.6 | 1.9 | 65 | 60.1 | 24.9 | 25 | 115.5 | 47.8 | 85 | 170.9 | 70.8 | 45 | 226.4 | 93.8 |
| 6 | 5.5 | 2.3 | 66 | 61.0 | 25.3 | 26 | 116.4 | 48.2 | 86 | 171.8 | 71.2 | 46 | 227.3 | 94.1 |
| 7 | 6.5 | 2.7 | 67 | 61.9 | 25.6 | 27 | 117.3 | 48.6 | 87 | 172.8 | 71.6 | 47 | 228.2 | 94.5 |
| 8 | 7.4 | 3.1 | 68 | 62.8 | 26.0 | 28 | 118.3 | 49.0 | 88 | 173.7 | 71.9 | 48 | 229.1 | 94.9 |
| 9 | 8.3 | 3.4 | 69 | 63.7 | 26.4 | 29 | 119.2 | 49.4 | 89 | 174.6 | 72.3 | 49 | 230.0 | 95.3 |
| 10 | 9.2 | 3.8 | 70 | 64.7 | 26.8 | 30 | 120.1 | 49.7 | 90 | 175.5 | 72.7 | 50 | 231.0 | 95.7 |
| 11 | 10.2 | 4.2 | 71 | 65.6 | 27.2 | 131 | 121.0 | 50.1 | 191 | 176.5 | 73.1 | 251 | 231.9 | 96.1 |
| 12 | 11.1 | 4.6 | 72 | 66.5 | 27.6 | 32 | 122.0 | 50.5 | 92 | 177.4 | 73.5 | 52 | 232.8 | 96.4 |
| 13 | 12.0 | 5.0 | 73 | 67.4 | 27.9 | 33 | 122.9 | 50.9 | 93 | 178.3 | 73.9 | 53 | 233.7 | 96.8 |
| 14 | 12.9 | 5.4 | 74 | 68.4 | 28.3 | 34 | 123.8 | 51.3 | 94 | 179.2 | 74.2 | 54 | 234.7 | 97.2 |
| 15 | 13.9 | 5.7 | 75 | 69.3 | 28.7 | 35 | 124.7 | 51.7 | 95 | 180.2 | 74.6 | 55 | 235.6 | 97.6 |
| 16 | 14.8 | 6.1 | 76 | 70.2 | 29.1 | 36 | 125.6 | 52.0 | 96 | 181.2 | 75.0 | 56 | 236.5 | 98.0 |
| 17 | 15.7 | 6.5 | 77 | 71.1 | 29.5 | 37 | 126.6 | 52.4 | 97 | 182.0 | 75.4 | 57 | 237.4 | 98.3 |
| 18 | 16.6 | 6.9 | 78 | 72.1 | 29.8 | 38 | 127.5 | 52.8 | 98 | 182.9 | 75.8 | 58 | 238.4 | 98.7 |
| 19 | 17.6 | 7.3 | 79 | 73.0 | 30.2 | 39 | 128.4 | 53.2 | 99 | 183.9 | 76.2 | 59 | 239.3 | 99.1 |
| 20 | 18.5 | 7.7 | 80 | 73.9 | 30.6 | 40 | 129.3 | 53.6 | 200 | 184.8 | 76.5 | 60 | 240.2 | 99.5 |
| 21 | 19.4 | 8.0 | 81 | 74.8 | 31.0 | 141 | 130.3 | 54.0 | 201 | 185.7 | 76.9 | 261 | 241.1 | 99.9 |
| 22 | 20.3 | 8.4 | 82 | 75.8 | 31.4 | 42 | 131.2 | 54.3 | 02 | 186.6 | 77.3 | 62 | 242.1 | 100.3 |
| 23 | 21.2 | 8.8 | 83 | 76.7 | 31.8 | 43 | 132.1 | 54.7 | 03 | 187.5 | 77.7 | 63 | 243.0 | 100.6 |
| 24 | 22.2 | 9.2 | 84 | 77.6 | 32.1 | 44 | 133.0 | 55.1 | 04 | 188.5 | 78.1 | 64 | 243.9 | 101.0 |
| 25 | 23.1 | 9.6 | 85 | 78.5 | 32.5 | 45 | 134.0 | 55.5 | 05 | 189.4 | 78.5 | 65 | 244.8 | 101.4 |
| 26 | 24.0 | 9.9 | 86 | 79.5 | 32.9 | 46 | 134.9 | 55.9 | 06 | 190.3 | 78.8 | 66 | 245.8 | 101.8 |
| 27 | 24.9 | 10.3 | 87 | 80.4 | 33.3 | 47 | 135.8 | 56.3 | 07 | 191.2 | 79.2 | 67 | 246.7 | 102.2 |
| 28 | 25.9 | 10.7 | 88 | 81.3 | 33.7 | 48 | 136.7 | 56.6 | 08 | 192.2 | 79.6 | 68 | 247.6 | 102.6 |
| 29 | 26.8 | 11.1 | 89 | 82.2 | 34.1 | 49 | 137.7 | 57.0 | 09 | 193.1 | 80.0 | 69 | 248.5 | 102.9 |
| 30 | 27.7 | 11.5 | 90 | 83.1 | 34.4 | 50 | 138.6 | 57.4 | 10 | 194.0 | 80.4 | 70 | 249.4 | 103.3 |
| 31 | 28.6 | 11.9 | 91 | 84.1 | 34.8 | 151 | 139.5 | 57.8 | 211 | 194.9 | 80.7 | 271 | 250.4 | 103.7 |
| 32 | 29.6 | 12.2 | 92 | 85.0 | 35.2 | 52 | 140.4 | 58.2 | 12 | 195.9 | 81.1 | 72 | 251.3 | 104.1 |
| 33 | 30.5 | 12.6 | 93 | 85.9 | 35.6 | 53 | 141.4 | 58.6 | 13 | 196.8 | 81.5 | 73 | 252.2 | 104.5 |
| 34 | 31.4 | 13.0 | 94 | 86.8 | 36.0 | 54 | 142.3 | 58.9 | 14 | 197.7 | 81.9 | 74 | 253.1 | 104.9 |
| 35 | 32.3 | 13.4 | 95 | 87.8 | 36.4 | 55 | 143.2 | 59.3 | 15 | 198.6 | 82.3 | 75 | 254.1 | 105.2 |
| 36 | 33.3 | 13.8 | 96 | 88.7 | 36.7 | 56 | 144.1 | 59.7 | 16 | 199.6 | 82.7 | 76 | 255.0 | 105.6 |
| 37 | 34.2 | 14.2 | 97 | 89.6 | 37.1 | 57 | 145.0 | 60.1 | 17 | 200.5 | 83.0 | 77 | 255.9 | 106.0 |
| 38 | 35.1 | 14.5 | 98 | 90.5 | 37.5 | 58 | 146.0 | 60.5 | 18 | 201.4 | 83.4 | 78 | 256.8 | 106.4 |
| 39 | 36.0 | 14.9 | 99 | 91.5 | 37.9 | 59 | 146.9 | 60.8 | 19 | 202.3 | 83.8 | 79 | 257.8 | 106.8 |
| 40 | 37.0 | 15.3 | 100 | 92.4 | 38.3 | 60 | 147.8 | 61.2 | 20 | 203.3 | 84.2 | 80 | 258.7 | 107.2 |
| 41 | 37.9 | 15.7 | 101 | 93.3 | 38.7 | 161 | 148.7 | 61.6 | 221 | 204.2 | 84.6 | 281 | 259.6 | 107.5 |
| 42 | 38.8 | 16.1 | 02 | 94.2 | 39.0 | 62 | 149.7 | 62.0 | 22 | 205.1 | 85.0 | 82 | 260.5 | 107.9 |
| 43 | 39.7 | 16.5 | 03 | 95.2 | 39.4 | 63 | 150.6 | 62.4 | 23 | 206.0 | 85.3 | 83 | 261.5 | 108.3 |
| 44 | 40.7 | 16.8 | 04 | 96.1 | 39.8 | 64 | 151.5 | 62.8 | 24 | 206.9 | 85.7 | 84 | 262.4 | 108.7 |
| 45 | 41.6 | 17.2 | 05 | 97.0 | 40.2 | 65 | 152.4 | 63.1 | 25 | 207.9 | 86.1 | 85 | 263.3 | 109.1 |
| 46 | 42.5 | 17.6 | 06 | 97.9 | 40.6 | 66 | 153.4 | 63.5 | 26 | 208.8 | 86.5 | 86 | 264.2 | 109.4 |
| 47 | 43.4 | 18.0 | 07 | 98.9 | 40.9 | 67 | 154.3 | 63.9 | 27 | 209.7 | 86.9 | 87 | 265.2 | 109.8 |
| 48 | 44.3 | 18.4 | 08 | 99.8 | 41.3 | 68 | 155.2 | 64.3 | 28 | 210.6 | 87.3 | 88 | 266.1 | 110.2 |
| 49 | 45.3 | 18.8 | 09 | 100.7 | 41.7 | 69 | 156.1 | 64.7 | 29 | 211.6 | 87.6 | 89 | 267.0 | 110.6 |
| 50 | 46.2 | 19.1 | 10 | 101.6 | 42.1 | 70 | 157.1 | 65.1 | 30 | 212.5 | 88.0 | 90 | 267.9 | 111.0 |
| 51 | 47.1 | 19.5 | 111 | 102.6 | 42.5 | 171 | 158.0 | 65.4 | 231 | 213.4 | 88.4 | 291 | 268.8 | 111.4 |
| 52 | 48.0 | 19.9 | 12 | 103.5 | 42.9 | 72 | 158.9 | 65.8 | 32 | 214.3 | 88.8 | 92 | 269.8 | 111.7 |
| 53 | 49.0 | 20.3 | 13 | 104.4 | 43.2 | 73 | 159.8 | 66.2 | 33 | 215.3 | 89.2 | 93 | 270.7 | 112.1 |
| 54 | 49.9 | 20.7 | 14 | 105.3 | 43.6 | 74 | 160.8 | 66.6 | 34 | 216.2 | 89.5 | 94 | 271.6 | 112.5 |
| 55 | 50.8 | 21.0 | 15 | 106.2 | 44.0 | 75 | 161.7 | 67.0 | 35 | 217.1 | 89.9 | 95 | 272.5 | 112.9 |
| 56 | 51.7 | 21.4 | 16 | 107.2 | 44.4 | 76 | 162.6 | 67.4 | 36 | 218.0 | 90.3 | 96 | 273.5 | 113.3 |
| 57 | 52.7 | 21.8 | 17 | 108.1 | 44.8 | 77 | 163.5 | 67.7 | 37 | 219.0 | 90.7 | 97 | 274.4 | 113.7 |
| 58 | 53.6 | 22.2 | 18 | 109.0 | 45.2 | 78 | 164.5 | 68.1 | 38 | 219.9 | 91.1 | 98 | 275.3 | 114.0 |
| 59 | 54.5 | 22.6 | 19 | 109.9 | 45.5 | 79 | 165.4 | 68.5 | 39 | 220.8 | 91.5 | 99 | 276.2 | 114.4 |
| 60 | 55.4 | 23.0 | 20 | 110.9 | 45.9 | 80 | 166.3 | 68.9 | 40 | 221.7 | 91.8 | 300 | 277.2 | 114.8 |
| Dist. | Dep. | Lat. | Dist. | Dep. | Lat. | Dist. | Dep. | Lat. | Dist. | Dep. | Lat. | Dist. | Dep. | Lat. |
| E.N.E. | | | E.S.E. | | | W.N.W. | | | W.S.W. | | | [For 6 Points. | | |

Fig. 8. Table I.—(Bowditch) for finding the difference of latitude and departure on the course sailed. If course is found at top of page, work down; if at bottom of page, work up.

# AMATEUR NAVIGATION

latitude at time of sight. Fig. 8 is a reproduction of a leaf from Table No. 1 showing how it is used.

Take the sun's declination and the Equation of Time and correct them to time of sight. They are given in the Nautical Alamanac for Greenwich mean noon. The hourly differences are given in adjoining columns. Multiply these hourly differences by the number of hours it is before or after Greenwich noon and divide the sum by 60 (seconds), which will give the correction to be applied, according as it is before noon or after noon at Greenwich; also, as the quantity is increasing or decreasing daily.

Next find the polar distance, as previously explained. If the latitude and declination are both north or both south, subtract the declination from 90° for the polar distance; but if one is north and the other south, their sum will be the polar distance.

Now, add together the sun's true central altitude, the latitude at time of observation, and the polar distance and divide their sum by 2. From this half-sum subtract the altitude, which gives the remainder. Take from Table No. 44 the log. secant of the latitude, the log. cosecant of the polar distance, the log. cosine of

## TIME

the half-sum, and the log. sine of the remainder. Take half the sum of these logarithms and inspect the column of sines in Table No. 44, where the hour-angle, or apparent time, will be found in an adjoining column, either A. M. or P. M., as the case may be. If there is a difference between the logarithm sought and the one found in the column of sines, enter the table at the bottom of the page with the difference, which will give the proportional parts for seconds.

To this apparent time just found is added or subtracted the corrected Equation of Time, as directed in the Nautical Almanac, to convert it into mean time at ship. Now apply this time to the corrected Greenwich mean time. If the Greenwich time is the greatest, subtract the time at ship from it and convert the difference of time into degrees and minutes of longitude (Table No. 7), which will be named West. If the time at ship is greater than the Greenwich time, the ship will be in East Longitude.

Here is an example of a longitude sight. On June 18, 1910, about 8:30 A. M., an altitude of the sun was observed and the time noted by the chronometer. Chronometer slow 3 minutes 51 seconds. Ship was approximately in Latitude

# *AMATEUR NAVIGATION*

34° 00′ North, Longitude 73° 30′ West.
Height of the eye 10 feet.

| | | |
|---|---:|---|
| Observed altitude | 44° | 24′ |
| Corr. | + | 12′ |
| Corrected or true central altitude | 44° | 36′ |
| Latitude | 34° | 00′ secant |
| Polar dist. | 66° | 36′ cosecant |
| | 2) 145° | 12′ |
| Half sum | 72° | 36′ cosine |
| True altitude | 44° | 36′ |
| Remainder | 28° | 00′ sine |

Logs. taken from Table No. 44.

| | |
|---|---:|
| Log secant lat. | .08143 |
| Log cosecant P. D. | .03727 |
| Log cosine H. S. | 9.47573 |
| Log sine remainder | 9.67161 |
| | 2) 19.26604 |
| Log sine of app. time | 9.63302 |

Find apparent time in Table No. 44, column of sines.

| | | | | |
|---|---|---|---|---|
| Apparent time | 8h. | 36m. | 29s., | A. M. |
| Equa. time N. A. | + | | 42s. | |
| Mean time at ship | 8h. | 37m. | 11s., | A. M. |
| Green. mean time | 1h. | 27m. | 01s. | |
| Slow | | 3m. | 51s. | |
| Cor. G. M. T. | 1h. | 30m. | 52s., | P. M. |
| M. T. at ship | 8h. | 37m. | 11s., | A. M. |
| Long. in time | 4h. | 53m. | 41s. | |

Converted into degrees and minutes, Table No. 7:
73° 25′ West.

# TIME

(The beginner should bear in mind in working time sights that the logarithms are in *decimals*, while with time and degrees the fractional parts are sixtieths.)

| ° | H. M. <br> M. S. <br> S. T. | ° | H. M. <br> M. S. <br> S. T. | ° | H. M. <br> M. S. <br> S. T. | ° | H. M. <br> M. S. <br> S. T. | ° | H. M. <br> M. S. <br> S. T. | ° | H. M. <br> M. S. <br> S. T. |
|---|---|---|---|---|---|---|---|---|---|---|---|
| 1 | 0. 4 | 31 | 2. 4 | 61 | 4. 4 | 91 | 6. 4 | 121 | 8. 4 | 151 | 10. 4 |
| 2 | 0. 8 | 32 | 2. 8 | 62 | 4. 8 | 92 | 6. 8 | 122 | 8. 8 | 152 | 10. 8 |
| 3 | 0.12 | 33 | 2.12 | 63 | 4.12 | 93 | 6.12 | 123 | 8.12 | 153 | 10.12 |
| 4 | 0.16 | 34 | 2.16 | 64 | 4.16 | 94 | 6.16 | 124 | 8.16 | 154 | 10.16 |
| 5 | 0.20 | 35 | 2.20 | 65 | 4.20 | 95 | 6.20 | 125 | 8.20 | 155 | 10.20 |
| 6 | 0.24 | 36 | 2.24 | 66 | 4.24 | 96 | 6.24 | 126 | 8.24 | 156 | 10.24 |
| 7 | 0.28 | 37 | 2.28 | 67 | 4.28 | 97 | 6.28 | 127 | 8.28 | 157 | 10.28 |
| 8 | 0.32 | 38 | 2.32 | 68 | 4.32 | 98 | 6.32 | 128 | 8.32 | 158 | 10.32 |
| 9 | 0.36 | 39 | 2.36 | 69 | 4.36 | 99 | 6.36 | 129 | 8.36 | 159 | 10.36 |
| 10 | 0.40 | 40 | 2.40 | 70 | 4.40 | 100 | 6.40 | 130 | 8.40 | 160 | 10.40 |
| 11 | 0.44 | 41 | 2.44 | 71 | 4.44 | 101 | 6.44 | 131 | 8.44 | 161 | 10.44 |
| 12 | 0.48 | 42 | 2.48 | 72 | 4.48 | 102 | 6.48 | 132 | 8.48 | 162 | 10.48 |
| 13 | 0.52 | 43 | 2.52 | 73 | 4.52 | 103 | 6.52 | 133 | 8.52 | 163 | 10.52 |
| 14 | 0.56 | 44 | 2.56 | 74 | 4.56 | 104 | 6.56 | 134 | 8.56 | 164 | 10.56 |
| 15 | 1. 0 | 45 | 3. 0 | 75 | 5. 0 | 105 | 7. 0 | 135 | 9. 0 | 165 | 11. 0 |
| 16 | 1. 4 | 46 | 3. 4 | 76 | 5. 4 | 106 | 7. 4 | 136 | 9. 4 | 166 | 11. 4 |
| 17 | 1. 8 | 47 | 3. 8 | 77 | 5. 8 | 107 | 7. 8 | 137 | 9. 8 | 167 | 11. 8 |
| 18 | 1.12 | 48 | 3.12 | 78 | 5.12 | 108 | 7.12 | 138 | 9.12 | 168 | 11.12 |
| 19 | 1.16 | 49 | 3.16 | 79 | 5.16 | 109 | 7.16 | 139 | 9.16 | 169 | 11.16 |
| 20 | 1.20 | 50 | 3.20 | 80 | 5.20 | 110 | 7.20 | 140 | 9.20 | 170 | 11.20 |
| 21 | 1.24 | 51 | 3.24 | 81 | 5.24 | 111 | 7.24 | 141 | 9.24 | 171 | 11.24 |
| 22 | 1.28 | 52 | 3.28 | 82 | 5.28 | 112 | 7.28 | 142 | 9.28 | 172 | 11.28 |
| 23 | 1.32 | 53 | 3.32 | 83 | 5.32 | 113 | 7.32 | 143 | 9.32 | 173 | 11.32 |
| 24 | 1.36 | 54 | 3.36 | 84 | 5.36 | 114 | 7.36 | 144 | 9.36 | 174 | 11.36 |
| 25 | 1.40 | 55 | 3.40 | 85 | 5.40 | 115 | 7.40 | 145 | 9.40 | 175 | 11.40 |
| 26 | 1.44 | 56 | 3.44 | 86 | 5.44 | 116 | 7.44 | 146 | 9.44 | 176 | 11.44 |
| 27 | 1.48 | 57 | 3.48 | 87 | 5.48 | 117 | 7.48 | 147 | 9.48 | 177 | 11.48 |
| 28 | 1.52 | 58 | 3.52 | 88 | 5.52 | 118 | 7.52 | 148 | 9.52 | 178 | 11.52 |
| 29 | 1.56 | 59 | 3.56 | 89 | 5.56 | 119 | 7.56 | 149 | 9.56 | 179 | 11.56 |
| 30 | 2. 0 | 60 | 4. 0 | 90 | 6. 0 | 120 | 8. 0 | 150 | 10. 0 | 180 | 12. 0 |

Table No. 7.—(Bowditch) for reducing longitude into time, and the contrary.

Here is an example of an afternoon sight for longitude, taken about 5 P. M., August 12, 1910 in North lat.:

| | |
|---|---|
| Observed altitude | 21° 13' |
| Correction | + 10' |
| Cor. alt. ............................. | 21° 23' |

# *AMATEUR NAVIGATION*

| | | |
|---|---|---|
| Lat. by D. R. .................... | 31° | 50' secant |
| Polar distance ................. | 74° | 57' cosecant |

$\phantom{xxxxxxxxxxxxxxxxxxxxxxx}$ 2)128° 10'

| | | |
|---|---|---|
| Half sum ........................ | 64° | 05' cosine |
| True alt. ........................ | 21° | 23' |

Remainder ........................ 42° 42' sine

Logs. from Table No. 44.

Log secant lat. ............................... .07079
Log cosecant P. D. ........................... .01516
Log cosine H. S. ............................. 9.64054
Log sine remainder .......................... 9.83133

$\phantom{xxxxxxxxxxxxxxxxxxxxxxxxx}$ 2)19.55782

Log sine of app. time ....................... 9.77891
From Table No. 44.
Apparent time .............. 4h. 55m. 34s., P.M.
Equa. of time (from N. A.) .... + 4m. 57s.

Mean time at ship.............. 5h. 00m. 31s., P. M.

Green. mean time............... 9h. 49m. 25s.,
Chron. slow................... 6m. 08s.

Cor. Green, M. T............... 9h. 55m. 33s., P. M.
Mean time at ship.............. 5h. 00m. 31s., P. M.

Long. in time.................. 4h. 55m. 02s.
Converted into degrees and minutes, Table No. 7:
73° 45' 30" West.

## Sight for Longitude taken about 8:30 A. M., February 2, 1911, in North lat.:

| | | |
|---|---|---|
| Obs. alt....................... | 23° | 42' |
| Correction ................... | + | 10' |
| Cor. alt...................... | 23° | 52' |
| Lat. by acc't ................ | 23° | 57' secant |

# *TIME*

Polar dist....90°
Sun's d'l, S. 17° 02'.................107° 02' cosecant
──────────────
2)154° 51'

Half sum....................... 77° 25' cosine
Cor. alt........................ 23° 52'
──────────────
Remainder                       53° 33' sine

Logs from Table No. 44:

Secant lat......................................... .03910
Cosecant P. D..................................... .01948
Cosine H. S....................................... 9.33818
Sine remainder.................................... 9.90546
──────────────
2) 19.30222
Sine of app. time................................. 9.65111
From Table No. 44:
App. time at ship.................. 8h. 27m. 10s.
Equation of time..................+  13m. 48s.
──────────────
Mean time at ship................ 8h. 40m. 58s., A. M.
Green. M. time................... 1h. 28m. 09s.
Chron. slow......................    10m. 29s.
──────────────
Cor. Green. M. T................. 1h. 38m. 38s., P. M.
Mean time at ship................ 8h. 40m. 58s., A. M.
──────────────
4h. 57m. 40s. W.

Converted into degrees and minutes of longitude by Table No. 7:

74° 25' West.

It may be well to explain further the use of Table No. 44. In the first example for longitude we require the secant of the latitude, which is 34° 00'. On page 642 we find 34° at the top left-hand corner. In the column

## AMATEUR NAVIGATION

marked "secant" we find the logarithms 10.08143. The 10 may be discarded, the decimal number alone being used. We next seek the cosecant of the polar distance, 66° 36', which is found on page 631. In the lower right-hand corner we find 66°, and, following up the column of minutes on the same side, we come to 36', taking from the column of cosecants adjoining the logarithm 10.03727, discarding the 10 as before.

Next find the cosine of the half-sum 72° 36', on page 625, in the same way. This is found to be 9.47573, keeping the whole number. The sine of the remainder, 28° 00', is found on page 636 to be 9.67161, retaining the whole number. We next take one-half of their sum, 9.63302, which is the sine of the apparent time, and, entering the column of sines, we look for this number, which is found on page 633. The nearest logarithm here found is 9.63292 (see Fig. 9), which is a difference of 10, to be entered in the small table for proportional parts at the bottom of the page on the line marked A. This gives us 3 seconds of time. The sine 9.63292 gives us 8 hrs. 36 min. 32 sec., taken from the column marked A. M. at the top of the page as it is a morning sight. From this

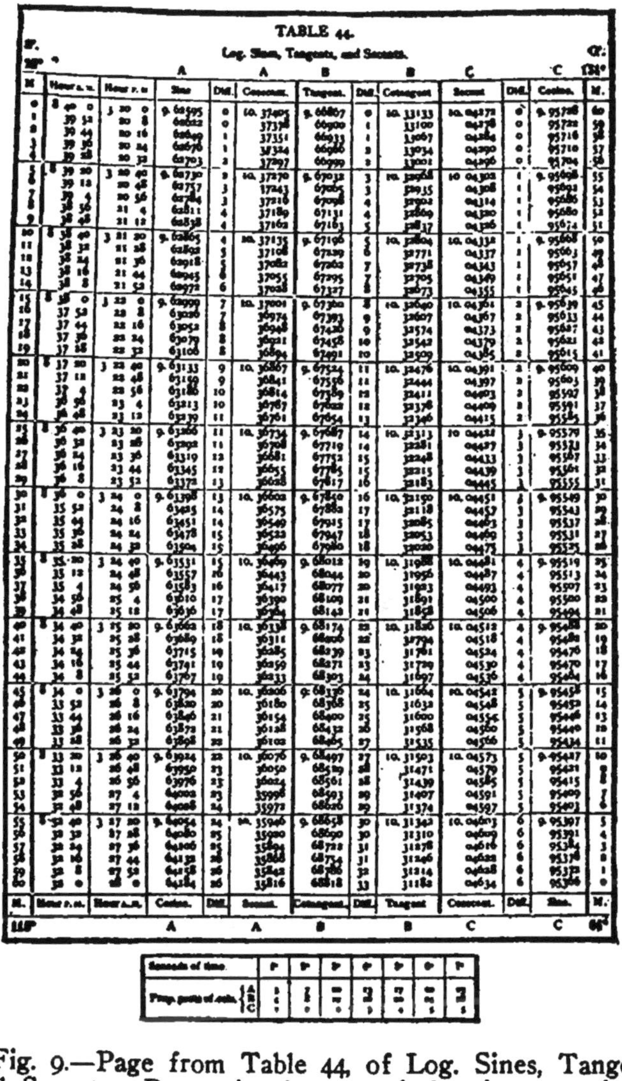

# TIME

Fig. 9.—Page from Table 44, of Log. Sines, Tangents and Secants. Proportional parts of the sines are found in the small table at the bottom.

# AMATEUR NAVIGATION

time subtract the 3 seconds found from the difference of the logarithms, which gives us 8 hrs. 36 min. 29 sec. A. M., the local apparent time at ship.

## SUNRISE AND SUNSET SIGHTS

Observations taken at sunrise or sunset are used for longitude, although large errors are liable to occur through refraction or imperfect horizon. To determine the longitude by this method, watch the sun's lower limb with a marine glass at either rising or setting, and at the instant it touches the horizon note the time by chronometer. Add together the latitude by account and the polar distance. From their sum subtract 21' and divide the remainder by 2, which gives the half-sum. Then add 21' (a constant used to allow for semi-diameter and refraction) to the half-sum, which gives the remainder. The Logarithms are now taken from Table 44 the same as in an ordinary time sight, and the apparent time at ship found, to which the Equation of Time is applied, converting it into mean time. Then the difference between mean time at ship and the Greenwich mean time will be the ship's longitude in time, which must be con-

## *TIME*

verted into degrees and minutes. When the sun's upper limb is observed, use 53' instead of 21' in the same way.

Here is an example of a sunrise sight taken January 2, 1911:

```
Alt. .............................................  0
Lat. by acc't................................  25°   30' N.
Polar distance..............................113°   00'
                                             138°   30'
Constant                                            21'
                                           2)138°   09'
Half sum..................................... 69°   04'
Constant                                            21'

Remainder                                    69°   25'
Log sec. lat....................................  .04451
Log cosecant P. D.............................  .03597
Log cosine H. S............................... 9.55301
Log sine remainder............................ 9.97135
                                           2)19.60484
                                              9.80242
```

From Table No. 44:
App. time........................ 6h. 44m. 57s.
Eq. time.......................+   3m. 48s.

M. T. ship...................... 6h. 48m. 45s.

Greenwich M. T.................11h. 36m. 30s.
Slow                              10m. 15s.

Cor. Green. M. T................11h. 46m. 45s., A. M.
Mean time ship.................. 6h. 48m. 45s., A. M.

Long. in time.................... 4h. 58m. 00s.
 Table 7 changed into longitude:
         74° 30' West.

## AMATEUR NAVIGATION

The beginner easily comprehends the theory and the practice in finding the latitude, but while being instructed in the method of finding the apparent time for longitude, the reasoning involved is not so clear to his mind. When told to put down the secant of the latitude and the cosecant of the polar distance, he naturally asks why it is done. The practical and experienced old navigator who may act as an instructor often does not know himself, but refusing to acknowledge the fact, gruffly replies to such a question, "Never mind why, but put it down."

Without knowing it, a problem in spherical trigonometry has been solved by the use of these logarithms, simply following the rules given for using the tables. The polar distance and zenith distance of the sun, and the co-latitude of the observer are the three sides of a spherical triangle, the value of the angle at the pole being the hour angle, or the local apparent time. Thus with the altitude, declination and latitude we can proceed to find the local apparent time.

In Fig. No. II M. Z. O. represents the meridian, E. Q. the equator, P. is the pole, and Z. the zenith, S. is the sun and S. H. is the

# TIME

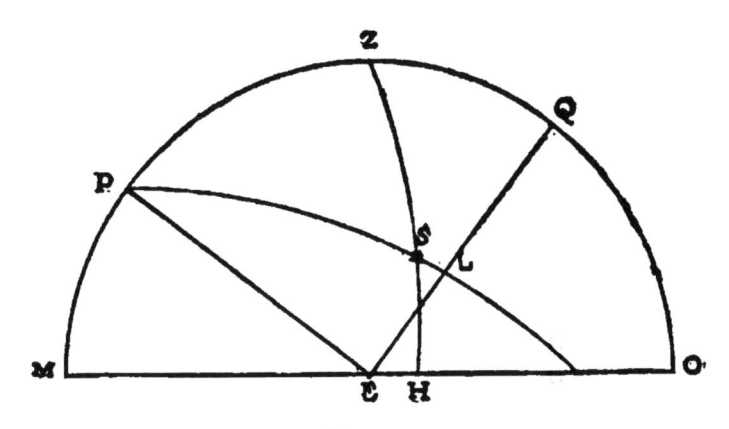

Fig. 11.

altitude. Therefore Z. S. is the zenith distance, S. L. is the sun's declination, S. P. is the polar distance, Z. Q. is the distance from the equator to the zenith (that is, the latitude); M. P. the distance of the horizon to the pole, is also the latitude. P. Z. is its complement, or so-called co-latitude. The three sides of this spherical triangle, Z. P. S., are now known and either of its angles can be found. The angle at the pole P. is the hour angle, which is the apparent time by the sun.

In the preceding examples, the calculations made in correcting the altitudes, declinations, equation of time, and chronometer time have been omitted for the sake of clearness in explaining each particular method. By spread-

## AMATEUR NAVIGATION

ing this work out, in full, an example becomes buried in a mass of figures, which is confusing. Practical navigators make the corrections mentally, or if writing them, use a spare paper without mixing them with the example proper.

With one exception, the examples which have been given for both latitude and longitude were in north latitude and west longitude. The problems have been used in actual practice at sea, proving their usefulness and correctness, and are better adapted to the use of amateurs in this vicinity than positions located in the more distant parts of the globe.

If one becomes a good navigator in the North Atlantic he will be equally good in the South Atlantic. The same rules apply there as here. The latitude will be reckoned from the South Pole instead of the North Pole, and if the sun bears north from the observer, the zenith distance will be named south and the declination applied to it as the rule and common sense indicate. In the working of a chronometer sight for longitude, calculate the polar distance from the South Pole.

In finding a position in east longitude the only difference will be found in the Greenwich time, which will there be earlier than the local

## TIME

time at ship. When a ship leaves New York and proceeds across the Atlantic, through the Mediterranean Sea or around the Cape of Good Hope, the local time becomes nearer the Greenwich time until the meridian of Greenwich is reached, when both times would exactly agree. Proceeding farther eastward, the sun would rise at ship's position before rising at Greenwich; therefore, the time at ship would be the latest and Greenwich time the earliest. Here is a little couplet of use in fixing this in the memory:

"Greenwich time best
Longitude West.
Greenwich time least
Longitude East."

Here is an example in South Latitude and East Longitude: On February 8, 1911, ship was approximately in Lat. 29° 55′ South, Long. 47° 00′ East. About 8 A. M. observed altitude of the sun was 33° 21′. Chronometer time 4h. 56m. 10s., slow 10m. 32s. Corrected equation of time 14m. 20s. to be added. Correct declination 15° 20′ South.

Obs. alt.................................. 33° 21′
Cor. .................................... + 10′
True alt................................. 33° 31′

# AMATEUR NAVIGATION

| | | | |
|---|---|---|---|
| Lat. | 29° | 55′ | .06211 |
| Polar dist. | 74° | 40′ | .01574 |
| | 2) 138° | 06′ | |
| H. S. | 69° | 03′ | 9.55334 |
| | 33° | 31′ | |
| Rem. | 35° | 32′ | 9.76441 |
| | | 2) | 19.39560 |
| | | | 9.69780 |

| | | | |
|---|---|---|---|
| App. time, ship | 8h. | 00m. | 42s. |
| Eq. of time | + | 14m. | 20s. |
| Local M. T. | 8h. | 15m. | 02s. |
| Chron. time | 4h. | 56m. | 10s. |
| Chron. slow | 0h. | 10m. | 32s. |
| Greenwich M. T. | 5h. | 06m. | 42s. |
| L. M. T. | 8h. | 15m. | 02s. |
| G. M. T. | 5h. | 06m. | 42s. |
| Long. in T. | 3h. | 08m. | 20s. |
| Long. | | 47° | 05′ E. |

The Local Time at ship is greater than the Greenwich Time, therefore the longitude found is East.

In traveling around the world in a westerly direction a day will be lost, while in an easterly direction a day will be gained. If one traveled westward with sufficient speed to keep the sun always overhead, he would return here tomorrow without having any night and apparently the same day. If he traveled eastward with the

## *TIME*

same speed, he would meet the sun, having a second day at the antipodes and a third day on arriving here tomorrow. The day begins at the 180th meridian; on one side of the line it will be Sunday, while it is Monday on the other side. Ships crossing this line to the eastward repeat one day, while ships crossing to the westward drop one day from the calendar.

# CHAPTER III

## THE SUMNER LINE

WE have shown in previous chapters how to obtain latitude by a meridian observation of the sun; also, how to find the longitude by morning and afternoon observations. Whenever a single observation is worked for either latitude or longitude, the ship's position is not determined definitely by it alone. Both of these observations are necessary by the methods there explained to find the ship's position.

In finding the latitude by a meridian altitude, the sun, or other body, bears either north or south from the observer, and the ship is known to be in a certain latitude; that is, somewhere on a line running in an east and west direction. The longitude is not determined by it. When an observation is taken for longitude at the time the sun is on the prime vertical (bearing east or west), the result will put the ship some-

## THE SUMNER LINE

where on a line running north and south—that is, on a line at right angles to the bearing of the body observed—as noted in the previous observation for latitude. If a ship's position is known to be on two such lines, one running north and south and the other running east and west, she must be at their point of intersection.

But it often happens that a meridian altitude cannot be obtained. The sun may be under a cloud at noon, or the horizon may be enveloped in a bank of fog. One cannot always wait until noon to find a position; yet it is necessary to know it, in order to proceed with safety, especially in vessels of great speed. Although one observation will not determine the exact position of the observer, it will give a line of positions, which may be all that is required at the time.

The sun is always at the zenith of some point of the earth's surface, and if an observer at this sub-solar point knew the exact time, east or west of Greenwich, at the same instant, his position could be calculated with exactness. This is true in theory, but as the sun is seldom or never in the observer's zenith, it is of no practical use in navigation. Whenever the sun is visible except in the zenith the observer will

## AMATEUR NAVIGATION

be somewhere on the circumference of a circle of equal altitude, the radius of the circle being equal to the zenith distance. For instance, if the sun's altitude is 60°, the zenith distance will be 30°, and the observer will be 30° from the sub-solar point, or point directly under the sun. Everywhere, north, south, east and west, 30°

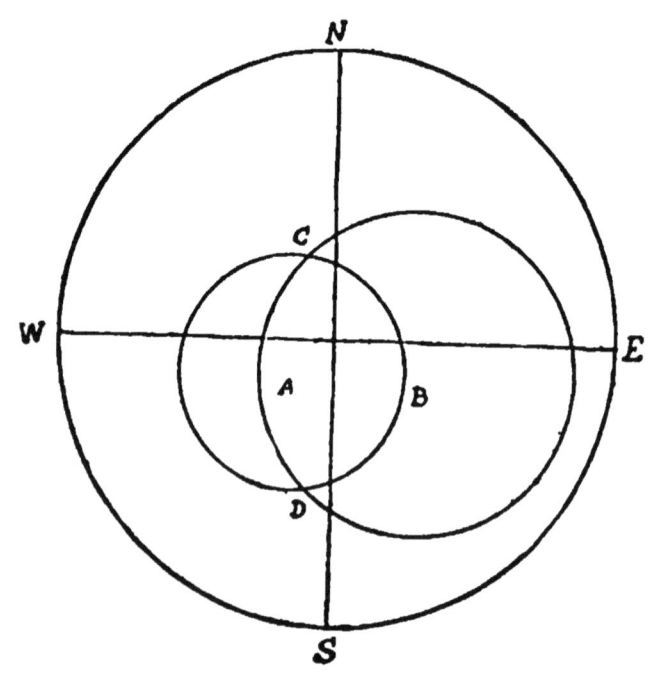

Fig. 12.—A and B are sub-solar points. Everywhere on circles equally distant from one of these sub-solar points observers obtain the same altitude at the same instant of time. The inner circles of equal altitude cut at C and D. As one is north and the other south of equator, there is no chance of error in finding position.

## THE SUMNER LINE

distant from this sub-solar point, observers would obtain the same altitude at the same instant of time. (See Fig. 12.)

The nearer the sun is to the zenith, the smaller the circle, while the greater the zenith distance, the greater this circle of equal altitude will be. The observer will know whether the time of his observation is in the forenoon or afternoon, and whether he is north or south of the sun; therefore, it is at once apparent on which part of the circle he is. He will also know the ship's position within one or two degrees, so that when a low altitude is taken for longitude the circle will be a large one, and the small portion used in finding a position on a chart will appear as a straight line. This line of position is called the Sumner Line.

If an altitude is taken for longitude and worked out with the latitude by dead reckoning, it will give a certain position. Now, by working the same sight with two assumed latitudes, one 30 miles north and the other 30 miles south of the latitude used in the first computation, two more points of position will be found. In plotting these three points on the chart, they will be found to lie in a straight line with one another. The ship is somewhere on this line,

## AMATEUR NAVIGATION

or its extension, at the time of the observation. Only two points are required to determine the direction of a straight line; therefore, the working out of the first position may be omitted.

If the true bearing of the sun is known at the time of observation, this process can be shortened again, and the line of position found by working the sight with the latitude by account, or an assumed latitude only. The ship's line of position is always at right angles to the bearing of the sun or other celestial body observed. This line of position is often of great value, especially when a ship is in the proximity of land, as this line, together with a sounding, may sufficiently define the position. If, on the Atlantic coast of the United States, a sight is taken with the sun bearing S. E., the line of position found will lie in a N. E. and S. W. direction, nearly parallel to the coast line. Again, with the sun bearing S. W., a line of position may be found running S. E. and N. W., which, if extended, will cut some prominent point of land, lighthouse, or lightship; and by steering a course on this line the objective point will be made right ahead.

When an observation is taken the sun's

## THE SUMNER LINE

bearing may be noted at once by the compass and corrected for variation and deviation to find the true bearing. A better way is to take the bearing from the azimuth tables. Enter the tables (either Burdwood's or Davis') with the approximate latitude, declination of the sun, and the apparent time, as found in working the sight, and the true bearing can be found at once. The sight must be worked using the latitude by account and an approximate position found. Plot this position on the chart, and draw a straight line through this point at right angles to the sun's true bearing. After the sun has changed its bearing at least two points, take a second observation and the sun's true bearing, and find another line of position, which must be drawn on the chart, as before. The point of intersection of the two lines will be the ship's position, if she has not altered her position between the times of the two observations. (The principle of this is shown in Fig. 13.)

In case she has changed her position, mark off the course and distance made in the interval of time between the two sights from the first line. Now draw a line through the point arrived at parallel to the first line. Where this

## AMATEUR NAVIGATION

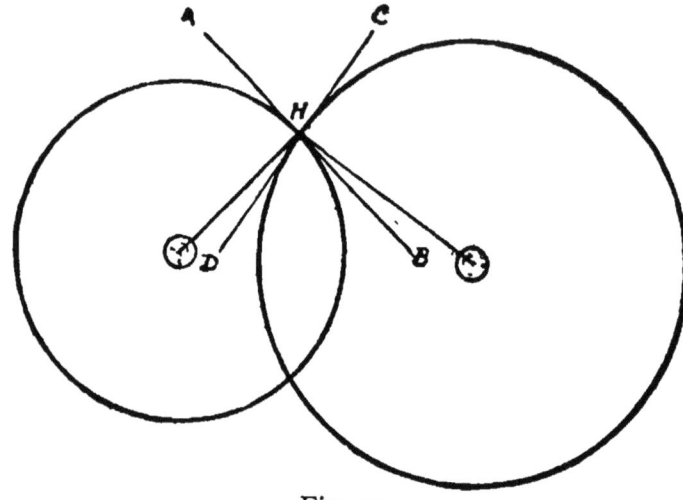

Fig. 13.

Fig. 13.—Circumference of circles of equal altitudes cut each other at H. Lines of position A B and C D, tangents drawn at right angles to bearing of the sun, coincides with circumferences at Point H.

line now crosses the second line will be the ship's position at the time of the last observation. The lines should cross as near at right angles as possible to better define the position. If the lines have only a slight difference of direction, the least error in calculation or plotting on the chart would cause a great error at the point of their intersection. (See Fig. 14.)

Fig. 14 is given to show how the line of position found is always at right angles to the bearing of the sun or other body observed. In the morning when the sun bore S. E. the line of

## THE SUMNER LINE

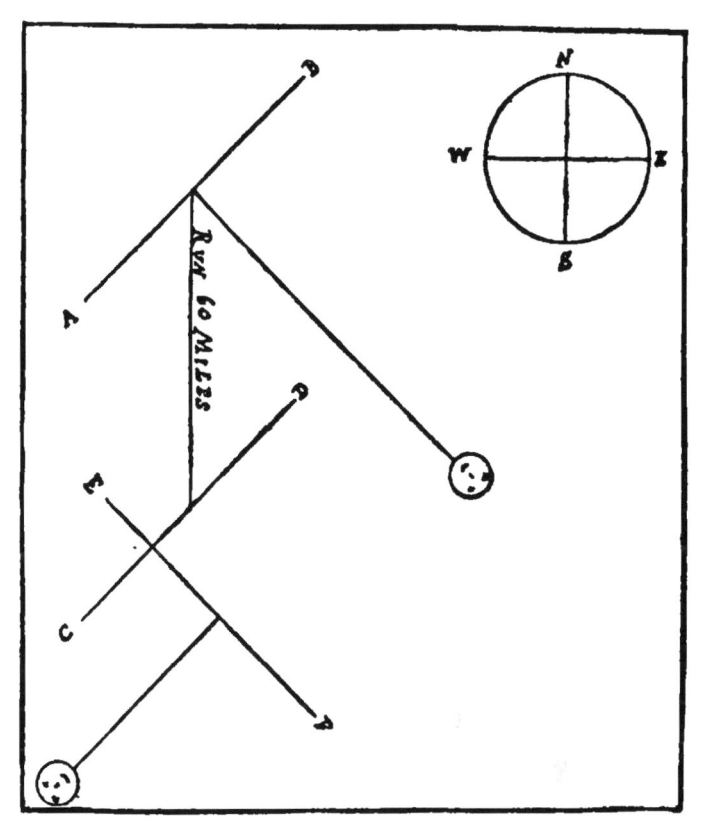

Fig. 14.—Sumner lines. In first sight line A B is drawn at right angles to bearing of the sun. After running 60 miles the second line of position, E F, is drawn at right angles to bearing of the sun. Line C D is then drawn parallel to line A B, representing the run of 60 miles made between the two sights. Where C D crosses E F is ship's position at time of last observation.

position A B was in a N. E. and S. W. direction. After a run 60 miles south the sun bore S. W. and the line of position then found, E F, ran N. W. and S. E. The line C D is parallel

## AMATEUR NAVIGATION

to A B distant 60 miles. Where C D crosses line E F is the ship's position at time of last observation.

Double altitudes, giving the two lines at once, are the best, as in the use of two planets, or stars, when at a large angle of bearing. Such observations are not reliable unless taken in the twilight, when the horizon can be well defined. Venus and Jupiter sometimes excepted, the sun only can be used in the daytime, all other bodies being obscured by its brilliancy.

Some examples of the use of the Sumner lines, in actual practice at sea, will now be given:

On March 3, 1911, about 7:26 A. M., ship was approximately in Lat. 24° 40′ N. and Long. 74° 10′ W. True altitude sun's center 16° 09′, the Greenwich mean time by chronometer 12h. 23m. 40s., chronometer slow 11m. 08s. Sun's declination 7° 08′ S. Equation of time 12m. 17s., to be added to apparent time.

The ship then sailed S. by W. 25 miles, when it was about 9:44 A. M., and another sight was taken. Sun's true altitude 44° 21′, Greenwich time 2h. 42m. 22s. P. M. Declination of sun 7° 05′ S. We wish to find the posi-

## THE SUMNER LINE

tion of the ship at the time of the second observation.

Both sights are worked out with two assumed latitudes, one 30 miles north and the other 30 miles south of the latitude by account, given in the example as 24° 40′ N. By entering the apparent time in Davis' azimuth tables, with the latitude and declination, the sun's true bearing at the time of the first observation was found to be S. 73° E., and at the time of the second observation S. 48° E. The lines of position will be at right angles to these bearings at the time of each observation. To prove that they are correct, the sights are worked out fully with the assumed latitude and line of position first drawn, without reference to bearings.

### A—FIRST SIGHT

| | | | |
|---|---|---|---|
| Cor. altitude | 16° 09′ | | |
| Assumed lat | 25° 10′ | secant | .04332 |
| Polar dist | 97° 08′ | cosecant | .00337 |
| 2) | 138° 27′ | | |
| Half sum | 69° 13′ | cosine | 9.55003 |
| Altitude | 16° 09′ | | |
| Remainder | 53° 04′ | sine | 9.90273 |
| | | 2) | 19.49945 |
| Sine of apparent time | | | 9.74972 |

# AMATEUR NAVIGATION

| | | | |
|---|---|---|---|
| Apparent time ......................... | 7h. | 26m. | 27s. |
| Equation of time...................... | + 12m. | 17s. |
| Mean time at ship..................... | 7h. | 38m. | 44s. |
| Greenwich mean time................. | 12h. | 23m. | 40s. |
| Chronometer slow..................... | + 11m. | 08s. |
| Corrected G. M. T................... | 12h. | 34m. | 48s. |
| Mean time at ship..................... | 7h. | 38m. | 44s. |
| Longitude in time..................... | 4h. | 56m. | 04s. |
| Longitude ............................ | 74° 01' West |

First position:
    Latitude ................................25° 10' N.
    Longitude ..............................74° 01' W.

```
Cor. altitude ................  16°  09'
Assumed lat.................. 24°  10'  secant    .03983
Polar dist...................  97°  08'  cosecant  .00337
                          2) 137°  27'
Half sum ....................  68°  43'  cosine   9.55988
Altitude ....................  16°  09'
Remainder ...................  52°  34'  sine     9.89985
                                      2) 19.50293
Sine of apparent time..........................  9.75146
```

| | | | |
|---|---|---|---|
| Apparent time ......................... | 7h. | 25m. | 12s. |
| Equation of time...................... | + 12m. | 17s. |
| Mean time at ship..................... | 7h. | 37m. | 29s. |
| Greenwich mean time................. | 12h. | 23m. | 40s. |
| Chronometer slow .................... | + 11m. | 08s. |
| Corrected G. M. T................... | 12h. | 34m. | 48s. |
| Mean time at ship..................... | 7h. | 37m. | 29s. |
| Longitude in time..................... | 4h. | 57m. | 19s. |
| Longitude ............................ | 74° 20' West |

Second position:
    Latitude ................................24° 10' N.
    Longitude ..............................74° 20' W.

# THE SUMNER LINE

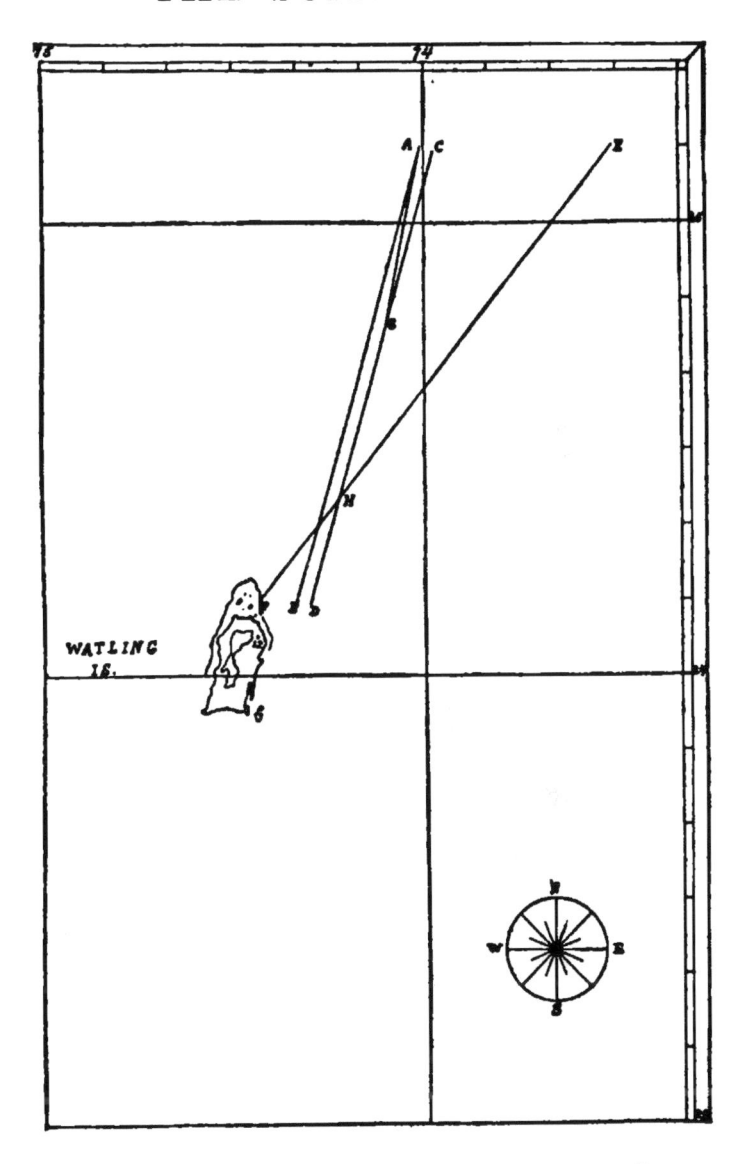

Fig. 15.—Method of finding position by Sumner lines.

# *AMATEUR NAVIGATION*

Plot these two positions on the chart. Draw a line connecting the two points. Ship is somewhere on this line or its extension. Sun's true bearing S. 73° E. Direction of line from *A* to *B* (Fig. 15) is found to be S. 17° W., exactly at right angles to sun's true bearing. Mark off 25 miles S. by W. from *A*, arriving at *G*. Draw line *C D* through point *G* parallel to line *A B*. Line *C D* will be the line of position at time of second sight.

### B—SECOND SIGHT

| | | | |
|---|---|---|---|
| Cor. altitude | 44° 21' | | |
| Assumed lat | 25° 10' | secant | .04332 |
| Polar dist | 97° 05' | cosecant | .00333 |
| | 2) 166° 36' | | |
| Half sum | 83° 18' | cosine | 9.06696 |
| Altitude | 44° 21' | | |
| Remainder | 38° 57' | sine | 9.79840 |
| | | | 2) 18.91201 |

| | | | |
|---|---|---|---|
| Sine of apparent time | | | 9.45600 |
| Apparent time | | 9h. 47m. | 10s. |
| Equation of time | | + 12m. | 16s. |
| Meantime at ship | | 9h. 59m. | 26s. |
| Greenwich mean time | | 2h. 42m. | 22s. |
| Chronometer slow | | + 11m. | 08s. |
| Corrected G. M. T. | | 2h. 53m. | 30s. |

## *THE SUMNER LINE*

Mean time at ship...................... 9h. 59m. 26s.

Longitude in time...................... 4h. 54m. 04s.
Longitude .............................. 73° 31' West
First position:
  Latitude ..............................25° 10' N.
  Longitude ............................73° 31' W.

Cor. altitude ....................44° 21'
Assumed lat..................24° 10' secant    .03983
Polar dist....................97° 05' cosecant  .00333
                              ─────────────
                        2) 165° 36'

Half sum ..................82° 48' cosine    9.09807
Altitude ..................44° 21'
                          ─────────────
Remainder ................38° 27' sine       9.79367
                                           ─────────
                                        2) 18.93490

Sine of apparent time................... 9.46745
Apparent time .......................... 9h. 43m. 30s.
Equation of time........................ +  12m. 16s.
                                        ─────────────
Mean time at ship....................... 9h. 55m. 46s.

Greenwich mean time..................... 2h. 42m. 22s.
Chronometer slow                        +      11m. 08s.
                                        ─────────────
Corrected G. M. T....................... 2h. 53m. 30s.
Mean time at ship....................... 9h. 55m. 46s.
                                        ─────────────
Longitude in time....................... 4h. 57m. 44s.
Longitude .............................. 74° 26' West
Second position:
  Latitude ..............................24° 10' N.
  Longitude ............................74° 26' W.

Plot these two positions on the chart. Draw a line connecting the two points. Ship is now somewhere on this line or its extension. Sun's

## AMATEUR NAVIGATION

true bearing S. 48° E. Direction of line from $E$ to $F$ (Fig. 15) is found to be S. 42° W., exactly at right angles to sun's true bearing. Line $EF$ cuts line $CD$ at $H$, which is the position of ship at time of second observation.

The position found by this method is Lat. 24° 23′ N., Long. 74° 16′ W. We will now work the last sight again, using this latitude.

```
Cor. altitude ................44°  21′
Latitude by obs..............24°  23′  secant     .04058
Polar dist...................97°  05′  cosecant   .00333
                         2) 165°  49′

Half sum ....................82°  54′  cosine    9.09202
Altitude ....................44°  21′

Remainder ...................38°  33′  sine      9.79463
                                              2) 18.93056
Sine of apparent time......................... 9.46528
Apparent time ......................... 9h.  44m.  12s.
Equation of time....................... +    12m.  16s.

Mean time at ship...................... 9h.  56m.  28s.

Greenwich mean time.................... 2h.  42m.  22s.
Chronometer slow                      +      11m.  08s.

Corrected G. M. T...................... 2h.  53m.  30s.
Mean time at ship...................... 9h.  56m.  28s.

Longitude in time...........................  4h. 57m. 02s.
Longitude ........................74° 15′ 30″ West
```

This is seen to get a result of 74° 15′ 30″, just one-half minute difference. None of these

## THE SUMNER LINE

calculations have been carried out beyond whole minutes, so the results are practically the same.

About half an hour after the last observation the lighthouse on Dixon's Hill, Watling's Island, was sighted bearing S. W. about 14 miles distant.

Over half the work we have done was unnecessary. Each sight could have been worked with the latitude by account to find a line of position. The line should be drawn through the position found at right angles to the sun's true bearing at the time of each observation. However, it is more satisfactory at times to do the whole work, especially if there is any doubt about the bearings of the objects observed.

Here is another example: On Dec. 31, 1911, position by dead reckoning Lat. 32° 08′ N., Long. 74° 40′ W. About 9h. 40m. A. M. sun's true central altitude was 25° 28′. Greenwich mean time by chronometer was 2h. 41m. 50s. Chronometer slow 31s. Sun's corrected declination 23° 10′ S. Equation of time 2m. 48s., to be added to the apparent time.

Ship then sailed south 58 miles, when at 3 P. M. another observation was taken. The true altitude of the sun's center was 20° 38′. Green-

# AMATEUR NAVIGATION

wich mean time by chronometer was 8h. 01m. 10s. Sun's corrected declination 23° 09′ S. Equation of Time 2m. 55s., to be added to apparent time.

We wish to find the position of the ship at the time of the second observation.

By using Burdwood's azimuth tables with the latitude, declination of the sun, and the apparent time at ship, the sun's true bearing at the time of the first observation was found to be S. 36° E. and at the time of the second observation S. 44° W.

First observation:
```
    Cor. alt.....................25°  28′
    Lat. by acc't................32°  08′  secant    .07221
    Polar dist...................113° 10′  cosecant  .03651
                              2) 170°  46′

Half sum ....................85°  23′  cosine   8.90574
Deduct altitude .............25°  28′

Remainder ...................59°  55′  sine     9.93717
                                        2) 18.95163

Sine of apparent time........................  9.47581
Apparent time ..........................  9h. 40m. 46s.
Equation of time........................  +   2m. 48s.

Mean time at ship.......................  9h. 43m. 34s.

Greenwich mean time.....................  2h. 41m. 50s.
Chronometer slow........................  +       31s.

Corrected G. M. T.......................  2h. 42m. 21s.
```

## THE SUMNER LINE

Mean time at ship...................... 9h. 43m. 34s.

Longitude in time....................... 4h. 58m. 47s.
Longitude ..............................74° 41′ 45″ W.
First position:
  Latitude ................................32° 08′ N.
  Longitude ..............................74° 42′ W.

Second observation:
  Cor. alt.....................20° 38′
  Lat. by acc't................31° 10′ secant   .06770
  Polar dist..................113° 09′ cosecant .03646
                        2) 164° 57′

Half sum ...................82° 28′ cosine   9.11761
Deduct altitude ..............20° 38′

Remainder ...................61° 50′ sine     9.94526
                                    2) 19.16703
Sine of apparent time........................... 9.58351
Apparent time ............................ 3h. 00m. 17s.
Equation of time........................+   2m. 55s.

Mean time at ship...................... 3h. 03m. 12s.

Greenwich mean time................... 8h. 01m. 10s.
Chronometer slow                                           31s.

Corrected G. M. T...................... 8h. 01m. 41s.
Mean time at ship...................... 3h. 03m. 12s.

Longitude in time....................... 4h. 58m. 29s.
Longitude ..............................74° 37′ 15″ W.
Second position:
  Latitude ................................31° 10′ N.
  Longitude ..............................74° 37′ W.

In Fig. 16 first position is at *P*. Sun's true bearing S. 36° E. Line *A B* is drawn through point *P* in a direction N. 54° E. which is at

# AMATEUR NAVIGATION

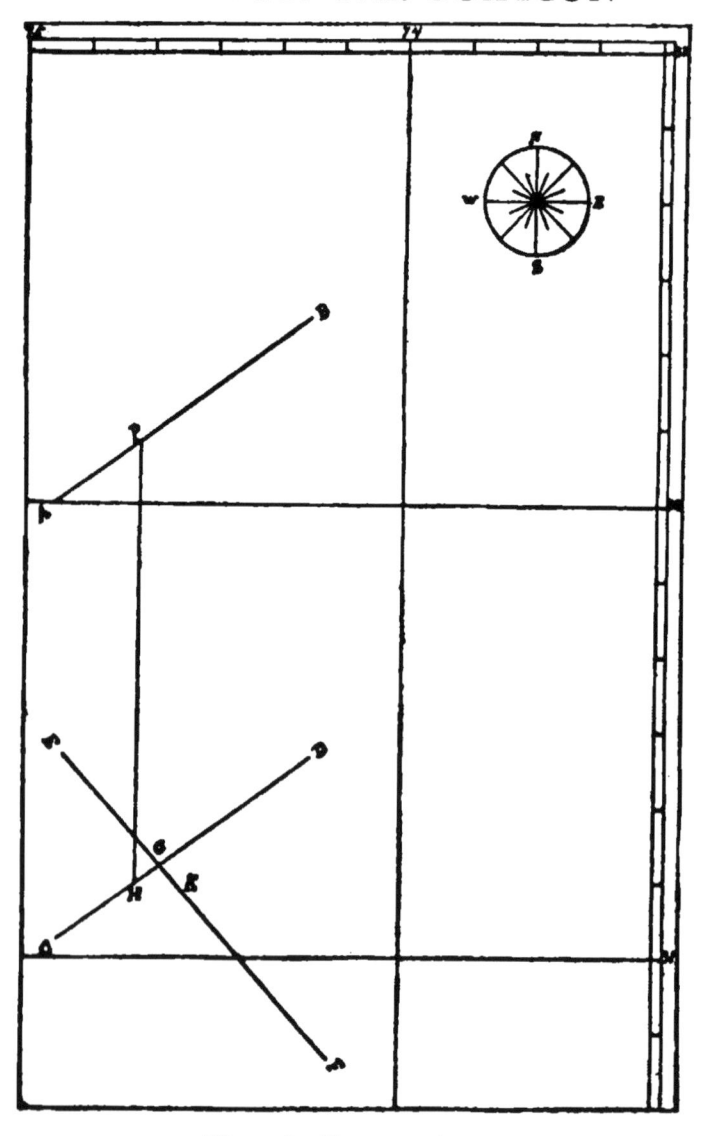

Fig. 16.—Sumner lines.

## THE SUMNER LINE

right angles to sun's true bearing. Ship then sailed 58 miles south arriving at point *H*. Line *C D* is drawn through point *H* parallel to line *A B*.

Second position was at *K*. Sun's true bearing at time of last observation was S. 44° W. Line *E F* is drawn through point *K* in a N. 46° W. direction—that is, at right angles to sun's true bearing. Now, where the line *E F* cuts line *C D* will be the position of ship at the time of the second observation—namely, at *G*, in Lat. 31° 12′ N. Long. 74° 39′ W.

This position can be found without drawing any lines on the chart. It is advisable, however, to draw the lines lightly with a pencil on the chart if the ship is near any dangerous shoals or coast line.

Another valuable use of the Sumner Line is shown in the illustration Fig. 17. A ship is running for the Brunswick Lightship and is found to be somewhere on the line *A A*. This line if extended would pass 10 miles N. W. of the lightship. If the ship is steered S. E. for 10 miles to line *B B* and then put on a S. W. course she must make the lightship directly ahead.

## AMATEUR NAVIGATION

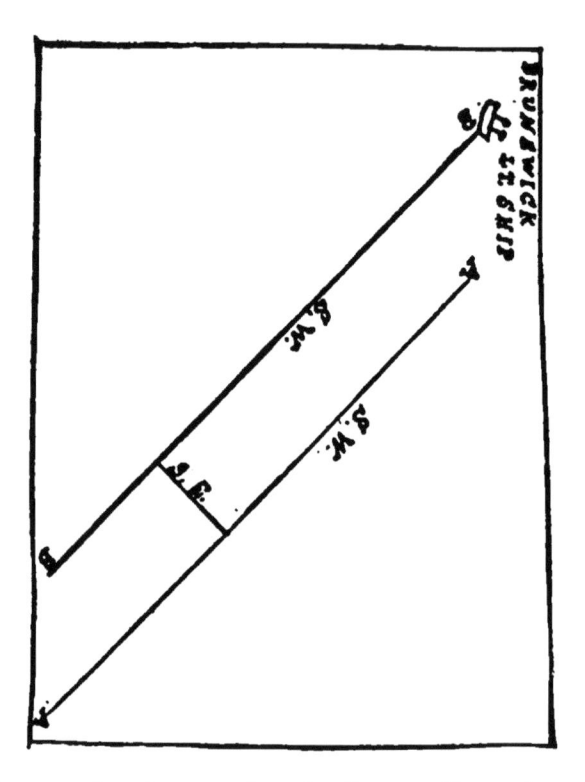

Fig. 17.—Another use for the Sumner line. A vessel is found to be somewhere on line AA, which line if extended would pass 10 miles N.W. of a certain point. If she steered S.E. for 10 miles to line BB and then is put on a parallel course to line AA, she will make the desired point directly ahead.

## CHAPTER IV

THE DAY'S WORK, EQUAL ALTITUDE, AND
EX-MERIDIAN SIGHTS

THE navigator calculates the position of his ship as accurately as possible at noon each day at sea, finding the latitude, longitude, course, and distance made from the previous noon, or from the last point of departure. It is customary to work the morning sight for longitude as soon as the observation is taken, using the latitude as found by dead reckoning. Unless the sun was on the prime vertical, or the latitude used proves to be correct, an error will occur in the longitude obtained. After the latitude is found by a meridian altitude at noon the latitude used in the morning may be corrected and the sight worked over again, in order to get the correct longitude at the time of observation.

Johnson's book, "Finding the Latitude and Longitude in Cloudy Weather," contains

## AMATEUR NAVIGATION

tables for making corrections to both latitude and longitude without working the sights over a second time, which are of great value in both shortening and simplifying the calculations for which they are intended. To correct the error in longitude as found by the morning observation by Johnson's table, proceed as follows: Find the sun's true bearing at the time of observation from the azimuth tables (Davis' or Burdwood's), using as arguments the latitude, declination and apparent time at ship. Then with the latitude and sun's true bearing enter Johnson's Table No. 1, and find there the error in longitude caused by each minute of error in the latitude. Multiply this quantity by the number of minutes the latitude is in error, and the result is the whole correction to be applied to the longitude.

It must then be known which way (east or west) the correction is to be applied. If the sun bears S. E., put it down thus: $\frac{S.}{N.}/\frac{E.}{W.}$ Then if the correction to the latitude is north, the correction to the longitude will be east, while if the correction to the latitude is south the correction to the longitude will be west. If the sun has a different bearing, put it down, as in this case, with the opposite bearing underneath,

## THE DAY'S WORK

drawing a line diagonally across from either N. or S., as is necessary. Practice in drawing the Sumner lines will make this at once apparent.

The following example will show this method more clearly. On January 17, 1911, at 8:30 A. M., ship was approximately in Lat. 26° 00′ N., Long. 74° 50′ W. Sun's observed altitude was 19° 20′. True bearing S. 52° E.

```
Obs. altitude  .............. 19°  20′
Cor.           .............. +    08′

True altitude  .............. 19°  28′
Latitude       .............. 25°  50′  secant    .04573
Polar dist.    ............. 110°  54′  cosecant  .02956
                         ────────────
                        2) 156°  12′

Half sum       .............. 78°  06′  cosine   9.31430
                             19°  28′
Remainder      .............. 58°  38′  sine     9.93138
                                                ─────────
                                              2) 19.32097
                                                 9.66049

Apparent time, ship................   8h.  22m.  08s.
Eq. time                              0h.   9m.  59s.

Mean time, ship....................   8h.  32m.  07s.
Greenwich mean time................   1h.  22m.  05s.
Chronometer slow                      0h.  10m.  26s

Cor. G. M. T.......................   1h.  32m.  31s.
Mean time, ship....................   8h.  32m.  07s.

Long. in time......................   5h.   0m.  24s.
Longitude        .................. 75°  06′   W.
```

87

# AMATEUR NAVIGATION

| | | |
|---|---:|---|
| Meridian altitude | 42° | 10' S. |
| | 89° | 50' |
| Zenith dist. | 47° | 40' N. |
| Declination | 20° | 52' S. |
| Latitude | 26° | 48' N. |
| Dist. sailed N | | 38' |
| Lat., 8:30 A. M. | 26° | 10' |
| Lat. first used | 25° | 50' |
| Error in latitude | — | 20' |

From time of observation for longitude, at 8:30 A. M., to noon, ship sailed 38 miles N. 3° W.
Sun's true bearing, S. 52° E. (Davis' Az. Tables).
Error in latitude used, 0° 20'.
Correction for each minute, 0'.87 (Johnson's Table I).
20 x 0.87 = 17.40.

Sun bears S. E. / N. W.

Correction to latitude is north; therefore, correction to longitude will be east.

75° 06' less 17' = 74° 49' W. corrected longitude.

Observation is now worked with the corrected latitude, proving the correction taken from Table No. 1 to be right.

| | | | |
|---|---:|---|---|
| Obs. altitude | 19° | 20' | |
| Cor. | + | 08' | |
| True altitude | 19° | 28' | |
| Latitude | 26° | 10' secant | .04696 |

# THE DAY'S WORK

```
Polar dist..................110°  54' cosecant   .02956
                         2) 156°  32'
Half sum ..................78°  16' cosine     9.30826
                             19°  28'
Remainder .................58°  48' sine       9.93215
                                             2) 19.31693
A. T. S. 8h. 23m. 15s...............................  9.65846
Apparent time, ship................... 8h.  23m.  15s.
Eq. time ............................. 0h.   9m.  59s.
Mean time, ship....................... 8h.  33m.  14s.

Chronometer time ..................... 1h.  22m.  05s.
Chronometer slow ..................... 0h.  10m.  26s.

Greenwich M. T........................ 1h.  32m.  31s.
Mean time, ship....................... 8h.  33m.  14s.

Long. in time........................4h.  59m.  17s.
Longitude ...........................74°  49'  W.
```

Thus the position at time of observation is Lat. 26° 10′ N. Long. 74° 49′ W. Ship then sailed N. 3′ W. 38 miles, making noon position Lat. 26° 48′ N. Long. 74° 51′ W.

Using the last example, the distance made good and the course from noon to noon are calculated as follows:

```
Jan. 17, noon....Lat. 26° 48' N.  Long........74° 51' W.
Jan. 16, noon....Lat. 22° 24' N.  Long........74° 36' W.
```
Difference in latitude 4° 24′   Difference in long. 15′
Difference of latitude=264 miles.  Difference of long.: 15′

# AMATEUR NAVIGATION

Enter Table No. 2 (Bowditch) where the difference of latitude and departure are given for 24 degrees, which is the middle latitude ship has sailed in. Enter 15 in the distance column and take out 13.7 from the latitude column, which is the departure made in miles. Now seek a course in the same table, where the difference of latitude 264 and departure 13.7 will agree. They are found to nearly agree on page 327, giving a course of 3°, which is our course, N. 3° W. Distance 264 miles.

Johnson's tables are very useful in finding the latitude and longitude simultaneously by means of two chronometer sights, which are calculated without drawing any lines on the chart. The method is there explained in the plainest manner, and numerous examples are given to illustrate the use of the tables.

### EQUAL ALTITUDES

A simple method of finding the longitude is by means of equal altitudes of the sun taken before and after noon. This method proves most reliable when the latitude and declination are of the same name and the sun passes near the zenith when on meridian. In such a case the sun rises and falls rapidly near the merid-

## THE DAY'S WORK

ian, and the time can be noted accurately within a few minutes before, and again after, noon. In other cases a longer interval of time is necessary, usually from fifteen to thirty minutes, in order to get good results, as in higher latitudes the sun changes its altitude very slightly when near meridian.

When the time is about as many minutes before noon as the lat. of ship in degrees, observe an altitude of the sun and note the time by the chronometer. Clamp the instrument, keeping it set on the same altitude, or else carefully take the reading and set it exactly the same again after taking the meridian altitude for latitude. Now with the sextant already set, watch the sun after passing meridian until its lower limb again touches the horizon, carefully noting the time by chronometer. Add the times by chronometer together and divide their sum by 2, which gives Greenwich mean time. Apply the equation of time as directed in the Nautical Almanac to obtain the Greenwich apparent time. The local apparent time at ship will be 12 o'clock, noon. Therefore, the Greenwich apparent time will be the longitude at ship in time. Reduce this time to degrees and minutes by Table No. 7.

# *AMATEUR NAVIGATION.*

In case the ship has sailed a considerable distance north or south during the interval of time between the two observations, a correction must be applied to the altitude before taking the time after noon. If the ship has sailed toward the sun, increase the altitude as many minutes as the ship has sailed in miles. If she has sailed away from the sun, decrease the altitude in a like manner before noting the time by chronometer after noon. Here is an example:

On April 11, 1911. In latitude 34° 41′ N.

Sun's altitude A. M..............................63° 02′
Sun's altitude P. M..............................62° 56′

Ship sailed 6 miles north in interval between observations; altitude P. M. decreased accordingly.

| | | | |
|---|---:|---:|---:|
| Time by chronometer................... | 4h. | 32m. | 16s. |
| Time by chronometer................... | 5h. | 02m. | 08s. |
| | 2)9h. | 34m. | 24s. |
| Greenwich mean time................... | 4h. | 47m. | 12s. |
| Chronometer slow | 0h. | 12m. | 04s. |
| Corrected time ...................... | 4h. | 59m. | 16s. |
| Equation of time..................... | 0h. | 1m. | 16s. |
| Greenwich app. time................... | 4h. | 58m. | 00s. |

Converted in longitude Table No. 7:
74° 30′ W.

Monday, April 24, 1911. Equal altitudes taken near noon for longitude:

# THE DAY'S WORK

Chron. Times.

|  | 4h. | 33m. | 05s. | A. M. } Altitude |
|---|---|---|---|---|
|  | 5h. | 10m. | 55s. | P. M. } 79° 55′ |

2) 9h. 44m. 00s.

|  | 4h. | 52m. | 00s. |
|---|---|---|---|
| Chron. slow .......... | 0h. | 12m. | 57s. |

|  | 5h. | 04m. | 57s. |
|---|---|---|---|
| Equa. time............ | 0h. | 1m. | 46s. |

Long. time............ 5h. 06m. 43s.=76° 40′ 45″ W.

Chron. Times.

|  | 4h. | 37m. | 40s. | A. M. } Altitude |
|---|---|---|---|---|
|  | 5h. | 06m. | 30s. | P. M. } 80° 20′ |

2) 9h. 44m. 10s.

|  | 4h. | 52m. | 05s. |
|---|---|---|---|
| Chron. slow.......... | 0h. | 12m. | 57s. |

|  | 5h. | 05m. | 02s. |
|---|---|---|---|
| Equa. time............ | 0h. | 1m. | 46s. |

Long. time............ 5h. 06m. 48s.=76° 42′ W.

Chron. Times.

|  | 4h. | 35m. | 25s. | A. M. } Altitude |
|---|---|---|---|---|
|  | 5h. | 08m. | 15s. | P. M. } 80° 10′ |

2) 9h. 43m. 40s.

|  | 4h. | 51m. | 50s. |
|---|---|---|---|
| Chron. slow .......... | 0h. | 12m. | 57s. |

|  | 5h. | 04m. | 47s. |
|---|---|---|---|
| Equa. time............ | 0h. | 1m. | 46s. |

5h. 06m. 33s.=76° 38′ 15″ W.

## AMATEUR NAVIGATION

```
                 Chron. Times.
                    4h.  42m.  00s.  A. M. ⎫ Altitude
                    5h.  01m.  50s.  P. M. ⎭ 80° 40'
                 ─────────────────────
                 2)9h.  43m.  50s.
                 ─────────────────────
                    4h.  51m.  55s.
Chron. slow.......  0h.  12m.  57s.
                 ─────────────────────
                    5h.  04m.  52s.
Equa. time........  0h.   1m.  46s.
                 ─────────────────────
                    5h.  06m.  38s. = 76° 39' 30" W.
```

The examples given on April 24 are unusually good, as the conditions were favorable to use this method. The ship was within the Tropics; the declination of the sun was the same as the latitude; the sun was, therefore, rising rapidly until it reached the meridian, and then began to decrease its altitude as rapidly. The ship was sailing on a due west course, so that no corrections to the altitudes were necessary, as is the case when a ship is sailing in a north or south direction. In high latitudes the results obtained by this method are always questionable, and should not be relied upon too implicitly.

If sights are taken several hours apart, a correction equal to the change in the sun's declination during the elapsed time between the sights should be made.

# THE DAY'S WORK

## Ex-Meridian Altitude

When the sky is partly overcast so as to cause any doubt about obtaining an altitude of the sun on meridan, take an altitude as near noon as possible and note the time by chronometer. To the Greenwich mean time apply the equation of time as found in the Nautical Almanac, reducing it to apparent time. Then take the ship's longitude in time (which is the time of the sun's meridian passage) and subtract from it the Greenwich apparent time, as noted. The difference will be the number of minutes from noon. If a time sight has been worked in the forenoon and the local apparent time accurately known, that is sufficient, as it is only necessary to know the number of minutes before or after noon.

With the altitude observed and the interval of time from noon, the meridian altitude must be found. This can be readily taken from Tables No. 26 and 27 (Bowditch). First enter Table No. 26 with the approximate latitude and sun's declination, having regard to whether they are both of the same name (north or south) or of different names, and take out the variation in altitude for one minute from meridian passage. Next enter Table No. 27

## AMATEUR NAVIGATION

with the variation for one minute and the whole number of minutes from noon and find there the whole correction, which is always to be added to the observed altitude. Now, having the meridian altitude, proceed to find the latitude in the usual way.

The latitude found will be correct at the time of the observation. The distance the ship sails north or south during the interval of time from noon must be applied to find the latitude at noon. Here is an example:

On April 11, 1911, ship was approximately in Lat. 34° 40′ N., Long. 74° 30′ W. At 11h. 45s. A. M. the sun's observed altitude was 63° 02′. Time by chronometer 4h. 32m. 16s. Chronometer slow 12m. 04s. Equation of time 1m. 16s. to be subtracted from mean time. Sun's corrected declination 8° 04′ 55″ N. Required the latitude at noon.

| | | | |
|---|---|---|---|
| Time by chronometer | 4h. | 32m. | 16s. |
| Chronometer slow | 0h. | 12m. | 04s. |
| Greenwich mean time | 4h. | 44m. | 20s. |
| Equation of time | — | 01m. | 16s. |
| Greenwich apparent time | 4h. | 43m. | 04s. |
| Longitude 74° 30′ W. turned into time (Table No. 7) is the Greenwich time of noon at ship | 4h. | 58m. | 00s. |
| Difference equals minutes before noon | 0h. | 14m. | 56s. |

# *THE DAY'S WORK*

Enter Table No. 26 with latitude 35° N. and declination 8° N.
Variation of one minute 3.6".
Reduction Table No. 27 for 15 minutes=14' 30".

| | | | |
|---|---|---|---|
| Observed altitude | 63° | 02' | 00" |
| Reduction to meridian | | 14' | 30" |
| Meridian altitude | 63° | 16' | 30" |
| Correction for dip, refraction and semi-diameter | | 10' | 00" |
| True central altitude | 63° | 26' | 30" |
| | 90° | 00' | 00" |
| Zenith distance | 26° | 33' | 30" N. |
| Corrected declination | 8° | 04' | 55" N. |
| Lat. time of observation | 34° | 38' | 25" N. |
| Sailed north 3 miles | | 3' | 00" N. |
| Latitude at noon | 34° | 41' | 25" N. |

# CHAPTER V.

### Star Sights

STAR sights are often invested with a good deal of awe by the amateur, when, as a matter of fact, one of the simplest methods of finding latitude is by an observation of the Pole Star.  As stated in a previous chapter, the North Star is very near the celestial pole, and if it could be seen by an observer at the equator of the earth it would appear on the horizon—that is, without any altitude.  As the observer travels northward the altitude of the celestial pole increases exactly as the observer's latitude increases until the 90th degree is reached at the North Pole of the earth, where the North Star would be nearly in the zenith. Therefore the Pole Star can be used for latitude at any time when visible and the horizon is sufficiently clear.  This star appears to describe a tiny circle around the celestial pole, with a radius of a little more than one degree in

## STAR SIGHTS

length, so that twice during twenty-four hours—that is, when exactly east or west of the celestial pole—the true altitude will be the observer's latitude without any correction. When the star is directly above or below the celestial pole the correction amounts to 1° 11′, to be added or subtracted, according to its position.

The correction to be applied to the altitude varies according to the part of the circle the star is on at the time of the observation—that is, we must know its hour angle. In the appendix of the American Nautical Almanac are several tables to be used for finding the latitudes by altitudes of the Pole Star. The method is to reduce the time of observation to local sidereal time. From this subtract the star's right ascension, which will give the hour angle. With the hour angle and declination take out the correction from Table IV, which is to be added or subtracted from the altitude, according to the sign given. The result will be the latitude. Example: April 12, 1911, 7:20 P. M.

| | | | |
|---|---|---|---|
| Local apparent time | 7h. | 20m. | 00s. |
| Equation of time | + | | 55s. |
| Local mean time | 7h. | 20m. | 55s. |
| Reduction table No. 3 | | 1m. | 12s. |

## AMATEUR NAVIGATION

| | | | |
|---|---|---|---|
| Green. Sid. time | 1h. | 18m. | 17s. |
| Local Sid. time | 8h. | 40m. | 24s. |
| Right As. Polaris | 1h. | 26m. | 00s. |
| Hour angle | 7h. | 14m. | 24s. |

Table No. IV. Correction + 23m.

| | | |
|---|---|---|
| Obs. altitude | 38° | 40' |
| Refraction and dip | — | 05' |
| True altitude | 38° | 35' |
| Cor. Table IV | + | 23' |
| Latitude | 38° | 58' N. |

In the abridged form of the Nautical Almanac issued by the leading nautical stores will be found a table for correcting the altitude of the Pole Star at any time, with simple instructions how the correction is to be applied. All that is needed is the right ascension of the meridian and the star's altitude. The R. A. M. is found by adding the apparent time at ship to the sun's right ascension, taken from the Nautical Almanac on the given date.

Example: April 12, 1911, 7:20 p. m.

| | | |
|---|---|---|
| Apparent time ship | 7h. | 20m. |
| Sun's right ascension | 1h. | 21m. |
| R. A. of the meridian | 8h. | 41m. |

Correction for 8h. 40m., Table IV, + 23m.

| | | |
|---|---|---|
| Obs. altitude | 38° | 40' |
| Refraction and dip | — | 05' |

## STAR SIGHTS

True altitude ............................... 38° 35'
Correction ................................... + 23'
Latitude ....................................... 38° 58' N.

The latitude found in this way is only an approximate one. More rigorous methods are available for those who wish to use them, but their explanation here would carry us too far.

In order to determine latitude and longitude by observations of the stars and planets, it is necessary to use terms and quantities which are not needed in like observations of the sun—namely, right ascension and sidereal time, a brief explanation of which will now be given.

We have used mean solar time and apparent solar time—time reckoned by the daily course of the sun. Sidereal time is that time which is calculated by the stars, the length of a sidereal day being the time elapsed between the two successive transits of the same star over the same meridian. The stars are mapped out in the heavens much the same as cities and towns are located on the earth, the star's declination being the same as latitude and right ascension the same as longitude on the earth. The longitude, or right ascension of a heavenly body, is reckoned from the vernal equinox (first point of Aries) east to 360 degrees in the circuit

*AMATEUR NAVIGATION*

of the heavens, instead of 180° east and 180° west from the meridian of Greenwich, as used on a map of the earth.

The sun's position among the stars is found to be continually changing, every day apparently moving more to the eastward. These daily positions have been recorded by astronomers, and the path of the sun is found to be a great circle, called the ecliptic, which crosses the celestial equator twice during the course of a year and returns to the same position at the end of each year. The places in the heavens where the ecliptic crosses the celestial equator in March and September are called the vernal and autumnal equinoxes. The vernal equinox is the point in the heavens from which the position of all heavenly bodies are reckoned in an easterly direction throughout the circle of the heavens, and is usually expressed in hours, minutes, and seconds.

The sidereal day is nearly four minutes shorter than the solar day. Noon by sidereal time is the time when the vernal equinox crosses the meridian instead of the sun, as in a solar day. On March 20, the mean solar time and sidereal time will agree. As the sidereal day is nearly four minutes shorter than the solar

## STAR SIGHTS

day, the sidereal time gains about two hours each month, making a difference of exactly one day in the course of a year, the solar year having 365¼ days and the sidereal year having 366¼ days.

Stars which now rise soon after sunset will soon be found near the meridian at sunset, which shows how a day reckoned by the stars is shorter than a solar day, and also shows the easterly motion of the sun through the heavens.

Sidereal time may be converted into solar time and vice versa. The right ascension and declination of all the planets and stars of any use to the navigator are given in the Nautical Almanac; also, the Greenwich mean time of their passing meridian. The ephemeris of the brightest planets is given in separate tables for each month. The hour angle, of course, changes at the rate of 15 degrees each hour (sidereal time), making a circuit of the heavens in twenty-four hours. The sidereal time, or right ascension of the mean sun, is also given in the Nautical Almanac.

Meridian altitude of stars or planets can be used to determine the latitude by the same method as is used with the sun. To find the latitude by a meridian altitude of a star is the

# AMATEUR NAVIGATION

most simple calculation used in navigation. The declination does not change perceptibly for years, and can be used just as it is taken from the almanac; while for the planets, the hourly corrections to be applied are found in an adjoining column, as in the case of the sun.

### PRINCIPAL STARS AND CONSTELLATIONS

The chief difficulty is in getting a reliable altitude when the star is on meridian. A familiarity with the stars and planets is also desirable, so as to recognize them readily when seen. A brief study of the heavens with the aid of a star map will soon give one a knowledge of the outlines of the principal constellations and their brightest stars.

Everyone knows the Big Dipper, and that "the pointers" are directed toward the Pole Star. The curve of the handle, if extended, would pass through Arcturus and thence to Spica. At right angles to a line drawn from "the pointers" to the Pole Star will be found Vega and Capella, at about equal distances on each side of the Pole Star. Capella is easily recognized by its brightness and yellowish color, and by "The Kids"—three fainter stars

# STAR SIGHTS

near by, forming a small isosceles triangle. Vega, the blue star, is seen at the apex of a small triangle joined to a small parallelogram forming the constellation of Lyra. The constellation of Cassiopea lies on the opposite side of the Pole Star to the Dipper and at about the same distance away. It is formed of a zigzag of stars forming an imperfect W. Arcturus, Spica, and Denebola form an equilateral triangle. Extend the line from Arcturus through Denebola, and it will cut Regulus. The Pole Star, Vega, and Arcturus form a right angle triangle, the right angle being at Vega.

Orion's sheath and belt are nearly as well known as the Dipper. A line drawn in a N. W. direction through Orion's belt will pass through both the Hyades and Pleiades. This line extended S. E. from Orion will cut Sirius (the Dog Star, and brightest star in the heavens). The brightest star in the Hyades is the well-known reddish star Aldebaran. On either side of Orion, at right angles to the line previously drawn, are seen Betelgeuze, to the N. E., and Rigel, the white star, to the S. W. The "heavenly twins," Castor and Pollux, are found about half-way between Orion and the Dipper. Castor is a double star, although

## AMATEUR NAVIGATION

Pollux is the brightest. Altair is the brightest star in the constellation of Aquila, and is the center star of three which appear in a straight line with one another at equal distances and pointing directly for Vega. Antares, a bright red star of the first magnitude, is easily distinguished in the wonderful constellation of Scorpio.

Having become acquainted with the most conspicuous configurations in the sky, the others may be readily found when sought.

When recourse to the stars or planets is to be had for latitude, look up the times of their passing meridian in the Nautical Almanac and see which bodies will be near the meridian during the twilight, either morning or evening. Having decided which body to observe, find the exact time of its passing meridian. This time is given in the Nautical Almanac for Greenwich mean time, or it can be found by subtracting the right ascension of the sun from the right ascension of the star. For instance, we wish the time Sirius passes meridian on April 15, 1911.

Right ascension Sirius from N. A........6h. 41m. 13s.
Righ ascension Sun from N. A..........1h. 30m. 55s.
Sirius on meridian....................5h. 10m. 18s.

# STAR SIGHTS

When it happens that the R. A. of the star is less than the R. A. of the sun, add twenty-four hours to the star's R. A.

On March 20, 1911, Sirius crossed the meridian at 6:52 P. M. The declination of Sirius is 16° 36' S. The meridian altitude was found to be 43° 28', bearing south. The altitude is corrected for refraction and dip of the horizon only, which amounts to about 5 minutes, and is always to be subtracted from the altitude.

```
Obs. altitude............................43°  28'
Dip and refraction.......................  −  05'
True altitude............................43°  23' S.
                                         90°  00'
Zenith dist..............................46°  37' N.
Star's declination ......................16°  36' S.
Latitude ................................30°  01' N.
```

To find the longitude by an altitude of a star or planet, proceed as follows:

Take the corrected altitude, latitude, and polar distance and proceed the same is if working a sight of the sun. This result will be the hour angle, and must always be taken from Table No. 44 in the column of apparent time marked P. M. If the body is east of the ob-

## AMATEUR NAVIGATION

server's meridian, subtract the hour angle from the right ascension of the body; if west, add them together, the result being the local sidereal time. To the correct Greenwich mean time add the sidereal acceleration found in Table No. III of the American Nautical Almanac and the sidereal time of Greenwich mean noon, which gives the Greenwich sidereal time. The difference between the Greenwich sidereal time and the local or sidereal time at ship will be the longitude in time. The local mean time may be found and applied to the Greenwich mean time, as in finding the longitude by an observation of the sun.

On April 11, 1911, ship was in Lat. 35° 57′ N., Long. 74° 35′ W., approximately, at 6h. 45m. P. M. The observed altitude of Venus was 26° 57′, bearing west. Chronometer time 11h. 32m. 45s. Chronometer slow 12m. 04s. Declination of Venus 19° 17′ N.

```
Obs. altitude                      26°   57′
Ref. and dip..................    —    06′

True altitude................    26°   51′
Latitude ....................    35°   57′  secant     .09177
Polar dist...................    70°   43′  cosecant   .02508
                              2) 133°  31′
```

# STAR SIGHTS

| | | | | |
|---|---|---|---|---|
| Half sum .................... | 66° | 45' | cosine | 9.59632 |
| | 26° | 51' | | |
| Remainder ................... | 39° | 54' | sine | 9.80716 |
| | | | 2) | 19.52033 |

| | | | |
|---|---|---|---|
| Hour angle ................. 4h. | 41m. | 10s= | 9.76016 |
| Chronometer time ......................11h. | 32m. | 45s. | |
| Chronometer slow ...................... | | 12m. | 04s. |
| Greenwich mean time....................11h. | 44m. | 49s. | |
| R. A. M. Sun........................ 1h. | 16m. | 16s. | |
| G. S. T....................................13h. | 01m. | 05s. | |
| R. A. Venus........................... 3h. | 21m. | 42s. | |
| Greenwich hour angle.................... 9h. | 39m. | 23s. | |
| Hour angle ........................... 4h. | 41m. | 10s. | |
| Long. in time............................ 4h. | 58m. | 13s. | |

Converted into degrees and minutes:

Longitude ........................74° 33' 15" W.

The same longitude found, reducing it to local mean time, as follows:

| | | | |
|---|---|---|---|
| Hour angle ........................... 4h. | 41m. | 10s. |
| R. A. Venus........................... 3h. | 21m. | 42s. |
| R. A. of meridian...................... 8h. | 02m. | 52s. |
| R. A. sun............................. 1h. | 17m. | 28s. |
| Local Ap. T.......................... 6h. | 45m. | 24s. |
| Equa. time ........................... + | 1m. | 12s. |
| Local mean time...................... 6h. | 46m. | 36s. |
| Chronometer time ......................11h. | 32m. | 45s. |
| Chronometer slow ...................... | 12m. | 04s. |
| Greenwich mean time....................11h. | 44m. | 49s. |
| Local mean time........................ 6h. | 46m. | 36s. |

# AMATEUR NAVIGATION

Longitude in time...................... 4h. 58m. 13s.
Longitude ........................74° 33' 15" W.

The difference between the local sidereal time and the Greenwich sidereal time may be used to determine the longitude:

Chronometer time ....................... 11h. 32m. 45s.
Chronometer slow ......................     12m. 04s.
                                         ─────────────
Greenwich mean time.................... 11h. 44m. 49s.
R. A. M. S............................  1h. 16m. 16s.
                                         ─────────────
Greenwich Sid. time.................... 13h. 01m. 05s.

Stars H. A............................. 4h. 41m. 10s.
R. A. Venus ........................... 3h. 21m. 42s.
                                         ─────────────
Local Sid. time........................ 8h. 02m. 52s.
 or R. A. of meridian.
Greenwich Sid. time....................13h. 01m. 05s.
Local Sid. time........................ 8h. 02m. 52s.
                                         ─────────────
Longitude in time...................... 4h. 58m. 13s.
Longitude ........................74° 33' 15" W.

On April 30, 1911, ship was in Lat. 21° 10' N., Long. 76° 04' W., approximately, at 6:45 P. M. The observed altitude of Venus 30° 06', bearing West. Chronometer time 11h. 38m. 55s. Chronometer slow 13m. 10s. Declination of Venus 24° 20' N.

Obs. altitude .................  30°  06'
Cor. .........................   —    05'
                                 ─────────
True altitude ................   30°  01'

110

## STAR SIGHTS

| | | | |
|---|---|---|---|
| Latitude .................. | 21° 10' | secant | .03034 |
| Polar dist................. | 65° 40' | cosecant | .04040 |

2)116° 51'

| | | | |
|---|---|---|---|
| Half sum ............. | 58° 25' | cosine | 9.71911 |
| | 30° 01' | | |
| Remainder ............ | 28° 24' | sine | 9.67726 |

19.46711

Hour angle ................ 4h. 22m. 15s.= 9.73355
Chronometer time ..................11h. 38m. 55s.
Chronometer slow .................. 13m. 10s.

Greenwich mean time ..........11h. 52m. 05s.
R. A. M. Sun................... 2h. 31m. 14s.

G. S. T...................14h. 23m. 19s.
R. A. Venus................ 4h. 56m. 54s.

Greenwich hour angle.............. 9h. 26m. 25s.
Hour angle ................ 4h. 22m. 15s.

Longitude in time............... 5h. 04m. 10s.
    Converted into degrees and minutes:
Longitude .................76° 02' 30" W.


On May 12, 1911, ship was in Lat. 38° 30' N., Long. 74° 15' W., approximately, at 7:30 P. M. The observed altitude of Jupiter 17° 27' to the east of the meridian. Chronometer time 12h. 10m. 05s. Chronometer slow 13m. 34s. Declination Jupiter 12° 57' S. Equation of time 3m. 46s., to be subtracted from apparent time.

# *AMATEUR NAVIGATION*

| | | | |
|---|---|---|---|
| Obs. altitude | 17° | 27′ | |
| Ref. and dip | — | 05′ | |
| True altitude | 17° | 22′ | |
| Latitude | 38° | 30′ secant | .10646 |
| Polar dist | 102° | 57′ cosecant | .01119 |
| | 2) 158° | 49′ | |
| Half sum | 79° | 24′ cosine | 9.26470 |
| | 17° | 22′ | |
| Remainder | 62° | 02′ | 9.94607 |
| | | | 2) 19.32842 |
| Hour angle | 3h. | 39m. 54s.= | 9.66421 |
| Greenwich mean time | 12h. | 23m. | 39s. |
| R. A. meridian sun | 3h. | 18m. | 35s. |
| Greenwich Sid. time | 15h. | 42m. | 14s. |
| R. A. Jupiter | 14h. | 25m. | 07s. |
| Greenwich H. A. | 1h. | 17m. | 07s. |
| Star's H. A. | 3h. | 39m. | 54s. |
| Longitude in time | 4h. | 57m. | 01s. |
| Longitude | 74° | 15′ | 15″ W. |
| R. A. Jupiter | 14h. | 25m. | 07s. |
| Hour angle | 3h. | 39m. | 54s. |
| R. A. meridian | 10h. | 45m. | 13s. |
| R. A. sun | 3h. | 14m. | 49s. |
| Local Ap. time | 7h. | 30m. | 24s. |
| Equa. time | | 3m. | 46s. |
| Local mean time | 7h. | 26m. | 38s. |
| Chronometer time | 12h. | 10m. | 05s. |
| Chronometer slow | | 13m. | 34s. |

## *STAR SIGHTS*

Greenwich mean time .................... 12h. 23m. 39s.
Local mean time ........................ 7h. 26m. 38s.

Longitude in time....................... 4h. 57m. 01s.
Longitude .............................. 74° 15′ 15″ W.

Greenwich Sid. time..................... 15h. 42m. 14s.
R. A. M. or local Sid. T................ 10h. 45m. 13s.

Longitude in time ...................... 4h. 57m. 01s.
Longitude .............................. 74° 15′ 15″ W.

On May 12, 1911, in Lat. 38° 40′ N., Long. 75° 15′ W. at 8:10 P. M. The observed altitude of Arcturus was 49° 54′ to the east of the meridian. Declination 19° 39′ N.

| | | | |
|---|---|---|---|
| Obs. altitude ............. | 49° | 54′ | |
| Ref. and dip.............. | — | 05′ | |
| True altitude ............. | 49° | 49′ | |
| Latitude ................. | 38° | 40′ secant | .10746 |
| Polar dist................ | 70° | 21′ cosecant | .02606 |
| | 2)158° | 50′ | |
| Half sum ................ | 79° | 25′ cosine | 9.26403 |
| | 49° | 49′ | |
| Remainder .............. | 29° | 36′ sine | 9.69368 |
| | | | 2)19.09123 |
| Hour angle .............. | 2h. 44m. | 31s.= | 9.54561 |
| Greenwich mean time ..... | 13h. | 05m. | 34s. |
| R. A. M. S............... | 3h. | 18m. | 35s. |
| G. Sid. time.............. | 16h. | 24m. | 09s. |
| R. A. star................ | 14h. | 11m. | 38s. |
| G. H. A.................. | 2h. | 12m. | 31s. |

# AMATEUR NAVIGATION

| | | | |
|---|---|---|---|
| Star's H. A. | 2h. | 44m. | 31s. |
| Longitude in time | 4h. | 57m. | 02s. |
| Longitude | 74° 15′ 30″ W. | | |
| R. A. star | 14h. | 11m. | 38s. |
| Hour angle | 2h. | 44m. | 31s. |
| R. A. meridian | 11h. | 27m. | 07s. |
| R. A. sun | 3h. | 14m. | 49s. |
| Local apparent time | 8h. | 12m. | 18s. |
| Equa. time | | 3m. | 46s. |
| Local mean time | 8h. | 08m. | 32s. |
| Chronometer time | 12h. | 52m. | 00s. |
| Chronometer slow | | 13m. | 34s. |
| Greenwich mean time | 13h. | 05m. | 34s. |
| Local mean time | 8h. | 08m. | 32s. |
| Longitude in time | 4h. | 57m. | 02s. |
| Longitude | 74° 15′ 30″ W. | | |
| Greenwich Sid. time | 16h. | 24m. | 09s. |
| Local Sid. time | 11h. | 27m. | 07s. |
| Longitude in time | 4h. | 57m. | 02s. |
| Longitude | 74° 15′ 30″ W. | | |

From the above examples it will be seen that star sights are not intricate or difficult. The hardest part of this method of finding latitude and longitude is in getting a good horizon and in being able to locate the star with the sextant. The latter will become easier, however, with practice.

# STAR SIGHTS

## Sidereal Time

It is at first difficult to understand clearly the method of regulating the time by the stars, called sidereal time. Sidereal noon occurs at all hours of the day and night. When the place among the stars called the vernal equinox is in the zenith, it is noon sidereal time, and the time is then reckoned through twenty-four hours to the time of the next transit.

Astronomers use clocks called "sidereal clocks," and the time as read by them is always the hour angle of the vernal equinox. The sidereal time at the moment any heavenly body passes the meridian will be its right ascension. Therefore, in watching stars pass the meridian with a transit instrument, the time as taken by such a clock will be the right ascension of each body as observed.

The vernal equinox is a fixed point in the heavens, as is also the position of each fixed star, so that their relative positions in regard to each other remain unchanged. This is true except for a very slight change caused by "precession," which it is unnecessary to discuss in this place. The declination of stars also remains unchanged for years, and as the positions of all the principal stars have been proved

# AMATEUR NAVIGATION

by an untold number of altitudes and transits, a sidereal clock may be corrected by taking the time of their transits with accuracy. The earth makes one revolution on its axis in twenty-four sidereal hours with no appreciable difference for thousands of years.

## THE SOLAR SYSTEM

The sun is at the center of the so-called solar system. The planets in their order of distance from the sun are Mercury, Venus, Earth, Mars, Jupiter, Saturn, Uranus, and Neptune. The orbits of Mercury and Venus are within the orbit of the Earth, Mercury being so near the sun it is seldom to be seen, while Venus appears as a morning star just before sunrise, or as an evening star just after sunset. The moon, of course, travels with the Earth in its orbit about the sun, although the daily motion of the Earth on its axis causes the moon to rise and set the same as other bodies, coming to the meridian, fifty-one minutes later each day, on an average.

Mars, Venus, Jupiter, and Saturn are chiefly used by navigators, their daily positions with hourly differences being published in the Nautical Almanac in separate tables.

# STAR SIGHTS

## The Zodiac

Although the knowledge is not necessary, anyone practicing the art of navigation by observations of the heavenly bodies is naturally interested in knowing the signs of the zodiac, and the parts of the heavens they represent. As before explained, the ecliptic is the apparent path of the sun in its annual circuit of the Earth. It may be imagined as a great circle obliquely cutting the Celestial Equator at two places exactly opposite each other, that is, 180° apart. At places 90° from either of these points, the ecliptic will be 23° 27′ north or south of the Celestial Equator, it being at these points that the sun obtains its greatest declination in June and December. This is the time of both the longest and shortest days on the opposite sides of the Equator.

The zodiac is a belt encircling the heavens 16° wide, the ecliptic being its center. The zodiac thus extends 8° on each side of the ecliptic. It is divided into twelve equal parts of 30° each, called signs, and the sun passes through one of these signs each month of the year. Within this great belt are the orbits of the moon and all the brightest planets. The names

# *AMATEUR NAVIGATION*

of the twelve signs are Aries, Taurus, Gemini, Cancer, Leo, Virgo, Libra, Scorpio, Sagittarius, Capricornus, Aquarius, and Pisces.

### SIGNS OF THE ZODIAC

| | | | | | |
|---|---|---|---|---|---|
| 0. ♈ Aries – – | 0° | IV. ♌ Leo – – | 120 | VIII. ♐ Sagittarius | 240 |
| I. ♉ Taurus – | 30 | V. ♍ Virgo – – | 150 | IX. ♑ Capricornus | 270 |
| II. ♊ Gemini – | 60 | VI. ♎ Libra – | 180 | X. ♒ Aquarius | 300 |
| III. ♋ Cancer – | 90 | VII. ♏ Scorpio – | 210 | XI. ♓ Pisces | 330 |

The sun enters the first point of Aries in March, the path of the ecliptic then crossing the Celestial Equator at the vernal equinox. It enters the first point of Cancer in June at the time of the summer solstice, the sun then having its greatest northern declination. The Tropic of Cancer takes its name from this sign. The sun enters the first point of Libra in September, at the time of the autumnal equinox, the ecliptic then crossing the Celestial Equator as the sun proceeds on its course to the southward. When it reaches the first point of Capricorn, for which the Tropic is named, it is at the winter solstice, the place of its greatest southern declination (see fig. 18).

The first point of Aries is of most importance, it being from this point that right ascension and celestial longitude are reckoned.

## STAR SIGHTS

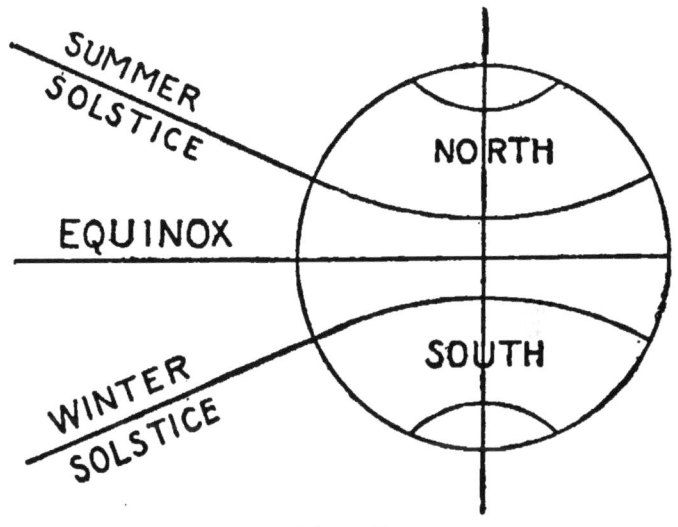

Fig. 18.

It may be mentioned here that the Arctic and Antarctic Circles are at the same distances from the Poles, that the Tropics of Cancer and Capricorn are distant from the Equator. The Polar Circles are in Latitude 66° 33′ North and South, which is **23° 27′** as measured from the Poles.

## CHAPTER VI

Some Hints on Taking Observations

WHEN particularly anxious for a position in long continued cloudy weather, take an altitude of any body which may show itself, taking the time and its bearing by compass. It will at least give a line of position which is always of some aid, by the use of Sumner's method, before explained, and may be all that is actually necessary for the time being. It is said that a poor sight is worse than none, like an inaccurate sounding with the lead. Yet an observation may be taken quickly and still be correct.

The sky is ever changing and usually some chance observation may be had if strict watch is kept. Set the sextant as nearly as possible to the right altitude and then watch sun, star, or planet as it issues forth from the slowly opening clouds. When the critical instant arrives, make a quick contact with the horizon

## TAKING OBSERVATIONS

and note the time. A long time looking at the horizon may give no better result.

There is a great difference in men in this proceeding. Among a group of ship's officers, one of them, by being prepared and alive to the necessity of the moment, may obtain a good observation, while others are fumbling with shade glasses and vainly trying to bring the object into their line of vision.

It is often convenient to use the sextant without the telescope when the sun is partly obscured by clouds. The reflection of both clouds and luminary are brought much more clearly to the eye. This is more especially of use for meridian altitudes, when an approximate latitude may be found even when the lower limb is not clearly defined, the sun being blurred behind thin clouds.

When a vessel is running on a north or south course, take an observation of a body bearing east or west, if possible, which will give a line of position running in the direction of the ship's course. If steering N. E. or S. W., choose some star or other body bearing S. E. or N. W. for the same object—to get a line of position in the direction of the vessel's course. This is one of the great benefits of using the stars and

## AMATEUR NAVIGATION

planets, as the navigator is not restricted to the use of any one body, but can select one suitable for the purpose required.

Some strange results are arrived at, in working sights at times, owing to refraction, false horizons, and the different density of intervening strata of the atmosphere. This is frequently noticed near the South Shoal Lightship off Nantucket, and on the northern edge of the Gulf Stream. A sort of mirage is noticeable, and at times a steamer's masts and funnel will be seen moving along in the distance, while below a clear range of sky lies between them and the horizon. Such conditions render altitudes taken totally unreliable.

It is a good practice to take two or three sights within a few seconds of each other, serving as a check upon errors in reading the altitude and taking the chronometer time. If the difference in altitude of two sights is not proportionate to the time interval, it is to be assumed that some error has occurred, and consequently another observation should be taken at once.

It is safer to make a large error than a small one, oftentimes. A flagrant mistake is evident at a glance and is easily detected, while

## TAKING OBSERVATIONS

a slight miscalculation may give one confidence in a false position.

All positions as calculated by observations at sea are approximate, that is, within a probable radius of two miles of the point determined. In a fast moving ship, the position may change several miles, while some intricate problem is being worked out. However, if the vessel's position is known within five miles by observation there is no need of getting into any difficulties.

Printed in France by Amazon
Brétigny-sur-Orge, FR